1 MONTH OF FREE READING

at

www.ForgottenBooks.com

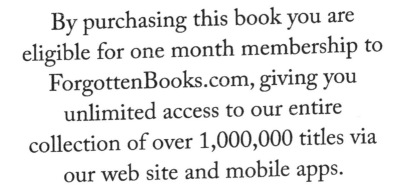

By purchasing this book you are eligible for one month membership to ForgottenBooks.com, giving you unlimited access to our entire collection of over 1,000,000 titles via our web site and mobile apps.

To claim your free month visit:

www.forgottenbooks.com/free992598

ISBN 978-0-332-29835-1
PIBN 10992598

This book is a reproduction of an important historical work. Forgotten Books uses
state-of-the-art technology to digitally reconstruct the work, preserving the original format
whilst repairing imperfections present in the aged copy. In rare cases, an imperfection in
the original, such as a blemish or missing page, may be replicated in our edition. We do,
however, repair the vast majority of imperfections successfully; any imperfections that
remain are intentionally left to preserve the state of such historical works.

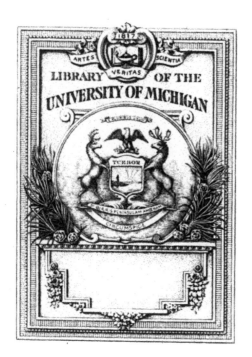

ELEVENTH BIENNIAL REPORT

OF THE

STATE AUDITOR

TO THE

GOVERNOR OF NORTH DAKOTA

July 1, 1908 to July 1, 1910

BISMARCK, N. D.
TRIBUNE, STATE PRINTERS AND BINDERS
1910

LETTER OF TRANSMITTAL

Office of the State Auditor,
Bismarck, N. D., October 15, 1910.

To the Honorable John Burke, Governor of North Dakota:

SIR: In compliance with law I have the honor to herewith hand you the eleventh biennial report of the state auditor, showing the condition of the state's finances for two years ending July 1, 1910.

Statements showing detail have been cut out, and accounts are shown in total in all cases.

In the back part of the report will be found a complete index to all the accounts listed herein.

Yours very truly,

D. K. BRIGHTBILL,

State Auditor.

AUDITOR'S DEPARTMENT.

D. K. BRIGHTBILL .... Auditor

CARL O. JORGENSON .... Deputy

EARL McCANNA .... Chief Clerk

M. A. SELVIG .... Bookkeeper

D. McPHEE .... Bookkeeper

HELEN McGILLIS .... Stenographer

PART ONE

ORDER ACCOUNT.

Receipts, disbursements and balances of all interest and income and permanent funds of the institutions and common schools. In the following statement all accounts are shown which do not depend upon legislative appropriation from the general fund for credit. All general fund accounts are shown in Part Two.

TOTAL ORDERS BIENNIAL PERIOD.

July, 1908	$ 76,883.20
August	120,268.15
September	92,748.71
October	240,602.21
November	97,221.08
December	78,513.34
January, 1909	84,382.99
February	213,571.43
March	128,272.46
April	264,989.24
May	375,192.81
June	171,166.70
July	221,152.29
August	101,927.43
September	543,637.81
October	254,558.69
November	188,572.22
December	276,376.61
January, 1910	198,787.23
February	227,410.77
March	130,885.51
April	364,270.69
May	795,291.75
June	113,580.83
Total	$5,360,264.15
General Fund warrants	2,543,567.88
Wolf Bounty warrants	71,362.67
Total cash payments all funds, biennial period	$7,975,194.70

PERMANENT FUND, COMMON SCHOOLS.

MONTH	Balance Fit of Mth	COLLECTIONS				Total Credit	Payments
		Sales Sutol Land	Redemption of Bonds	Payments on Mortgages	Miscellaneous		
1908							
July	$278,766.24	$12,037.16	$5,750.00	$900.00	$201.33	$297,654.73	$24,800.00
August	272,854.73		500.00	800.00	105.19	274,259.92	64,950.00
*August					193.71	193.71	872.00
September	208,631.63	3,552.00	5,100.00			217,283.63	61,900.00
ber	155,983.63	2,729.70	27,500.00	1,050.00	147.00	187,410.33	18,609.09
November	168,801.24	2,248.00	600.00	2,110.00		173,759.24	54,800.00
December	118,959.24	251,465.86	12,000.00	1,670.00	88,409.96	472,505.06	22,200.00
1909							
January	450,305.06	43,533.44	1,350.00	2,030.00	121.52	497,340.02	29,400.00
Féby	467,940.02	34,651.74	4,300.00	2,270.00	1,371.00	510,532.76	27,058.34
March	483,474.42	254,691.22	7,450.00	2,240.00	1,301.88	749,152	31,900.00
April	717,257.52	133.95	4,600.00	3,670.00		725,661.47	132,350.00
May	593,311.47	103,409.52	400.00	1,295.00		698,5199	87,160.70
June	611,255.29	363,424.62	2,150.00	940.00	70.56	977,8447	98,452.00
*June							633.26
July	878,755.21	2,617.73	7,150.00	130.00	103.97	888,756.91	18,532.00
*July							16,977.43
August	853,247.48	880.75	2,500.00	260.00	17.95	856,906.18	43,352.46
September	813,553.72	56,537.71	600.00	700.00	445.25	871,836.68	114,588.00
October	757,248.68	321.73	13,000.00	80.00	1,391.05	772,041.46	2,800.00
*October							400.00
November	618,841.46	1,845.20		1,590.00	430.75	622,707.41	105,700.00
December	517,007.41	59,928.14	200.00	690.00	26.15	577,851.70	124,500.00
1910							
January	453,351.70	2,291.20	1,700.00	2,210.00	168.83	459,721.73	129,946.45
February	329,775.28	186,154.70	2,900.00	3,160.00		522,289.98	46,700.00
March	475,589.98	267,029.75	2,700.00	1,000.00	19.25	746,428.98	84,200.00
April	662,228.98	46,728.42	11,750.00	1,430.00	1,012.09	723,149.49	64,950.00

May	658,199.49	45,574.48	5,150.00	1,005.00	2,755.36	712, 4683	115,800.00
June	596,894.33	810.86	2,500.00	1,650.00	1,423.68	603,268.87	18,950.00
July	584,318.87						
		$1,742,897.88	$122,050.00	$32,970.00	$99,516.48		$1,691,881.73

*Transfer.

July 1, 1908, balance ...... $ 278,766.24

COLLECTIONS—
Sales school land 1,742,897.88
Redemption of bonds 122,050.00
Payments on mortgages 32,970.00
Miscellaneous 99,516.48

Payments ...... $ 1,691,881.73
July 1, 1910, due 584,318.87

$ 2,276,200.60 | $ 2,276,200.60

PERMANENT FUND, STATE UNIVERSITY.

Amount expended from July 1, 1908, to July 1, 1910	$ 71,426.92	
Balance July 1, 1908		$ 3,774.63
Collections		81,610.06
Balance July 1, 1910	13,957.77	
	$ 85,384.69	$ 85,384.69

PERMANENT FUND, SCHOOL OF MINES.

Amount expended from July 1, 1908, to July 1, 1910	$ 32,981.02	
Balance July 1, 1908		$ 2,527.69
Collections		38,759.31
Balance July 1, 1910	8,305.98	
	$ 41,287.00	$ 41,287.00

PERMANENT FUND, AGRICULTURAL COLLEGE.

Amount expended from July 1, 1908, to July 1, 1910	$134,646.39	
Balance July 1, 1908		$ 21,646.01
Collections		135,213.87
Balance July 1, 1910	22,213.49	
	$156,859.88	$156,859.88

PERMANENT FUND, VALLEY CITY NORMAL.

Amount expended	$ 24,956.04	
Balance July 1, 1908		$ 1,767.98
Collections		51,447.26
Balance July 1, 1910	28,259.20	
	$ 53,215.24	$ 53,215.24

PERMANENT FUND, MAYVILLE NORMAL.

Amount expended	$ 19,173.63	
Balance July 1, 1908		$ 5,165.35
Collections		27,823.35
Balance July 1, 1910	13,815.07	
	$ 32,988.70	$ 32,988.70

PERMANENT FUND, SCHOOL FOR THE DEAF AND DUMB.

Amount expended	$ 24,976.45	
Balance July 1, 1908		$ 2,941.77
Collections		32,827.85
Balance July 1, 1910	10,793.17	
	$ 35,769.62	$ 35,769.62

PERMANENT FUND, BLIND ASYLUM.

Amount expended	$ 17,372.75	
Balance July 1, 1908		$ 3,640.04
Collections		25,137.02
Balance July 1, 1910	11,404.31	
	$ 28,777.06	$ 28,777.06

PERMANENT FUND, ACADEMY OF SCIENCE.

Amount expended .... $ 23,921.01
Balance July 1, 1908 .... $ 2,296.16
Collections 41,351.51
Balance July 1, 1910 .... 19,726.66

                                                 $ 43,647.67 $ 43,647.67

PERMANENT FUND, INDUSTRIAL SCHOOL.

Amount expended .... $ 20,715.99
Balance July 1, 1908 .... $ 328.13
Collections 36,490.26
Balance July 1, 1910 .... 16,102.40

                                                 $ 36,818.39 $ 36,818.39

PERMANENT FUND, SOLDIERS' HOME.

Amount expended .... $ 37,181.78
Balance July 1, 1908 .... $ 804.42
Collections 41,255.71
Balance July 1, 1910 .... 4,878.35

                                                 $ 42,060.13 $ 42,060.13

PERMANENT FUND, HOSPITAL FOR INSANE.

Amount expended .... $ 10,950.40
Balance July 1, 1908 .... $ 261.39
Collections 17,643.02
Balance July 1, 1910 .... 6,954.01

                                                 $ 17,904.41 $ 17,904.41

PERMANENT FUND, REFORM SCHOOL.

Amount expended .... $ 44,453.11
Balance July 1, 1908 .... $ 6,225.74
Collections 47,646.06
Balance July 1, 1910 .... 9,418.69

                                                 $ 53,871.80 $ 53,871.80

PERMANENT FUND—CAPITOL BUILDING.

Amount expended .... $ 1,349.48
Balance July 1, 1908 .... $ 70,251.04
Collections 46,400.57
Balance July 1, 1910 .... 115,302.13

                                                 $116,651.61 $116,651.61

INTEREST AND INCOME FUND, [COMM]ON SCHOOLS.

Month	Balance First of Month	COLLECTIONS					Total Credit	Payments
		Leasing School Land	Interest on Band Sales	Interest on Bonds	Interest on Mortgages	Misc'l Coll.		
1908								
July	$ 30,161.10	$ 5,487.93	$ 20,154.56	$39,305.34	$ 223.42	$ 358.50	$ 95,690.85	$ 150.60
August	95,540.25			4,667.68	221.33	97.49	100,526.75	1,807.86
September	98,718.89	2,618.92	7,307.78	739.36	85.46	3,236.50	112,706.91	12.36
October	112,694.55			4,671.25	323.33		117,689.13	94,549.70
November	23,139.43	11,020.75	4,883.93	1,935.15	4,874.30	102.50	45,956.06	22,916.32
Dember	23,039.74	1,293.40	7,856.98	4,948.72	5,050.32	12.00	42,201.16	399.77
1909								
January	41,801.39	5,045.94	5,662.26	45,971.25	3,467.21	10.00	101,958.05	105,165.92
February	101,958.05	1,104.10	5,117.62	3,559.02	7,553.66	65.00	119,357.45	1,793.10
March	14,191.53	14,587.69	145,619.81	3,425.18	1,932.62		179,756.83	
April	177,963.73			3,521.73	1,325.78		182,811.24	182,405.97
May	182,811.24	13,615.47	232,136.93	1,001.05	731.10		430,295.79	1,436.85
June	247,869.82	11,274.25	57,189.18	11,668.99	323.27	10.00	328,355.51	
July	326,918.66		16,977.43	40,526.34	67.83		384,490.26	
August	384,490.26			4,485.34	81.43		389,057.03	5,318.83
September	383,738.20	22,085.22	65,766.03	1,146.84	63.18		472,799.47	384,832.59
[Oc]ber	87,966.88	384.00	708.39	2,174.01	269.32		91,502.60	40.00
November	91,462.60	507.18	7,800.51	1,224.00	2,877.55		103,871.84	43.00
December	103,828.84	1,692.27	10,835.93	1,295.90	5,577.87		123,230.81	90,751.20
1910								
January	32,479.61	709.85	5,906.35	55,890.52	8,095.22		103,081.55	118.48
February	102,963.07	25,372.69	206,708.32	2,936.04	7,306.25		345,286.37	102,675.64
March	242,610.73	23,[B]89.17	284,153.35	5,583.32	3,232.66	10.00	558,779.23	2,634.90
April	556,[1]44.33	970.20	43,258.76	3,353.17	4,021.86		607,748.32	3,851.50
May	603,896.82	14,775.98	52,945.33	1,91.68	2,578.72		675,388.53	603,443.54
June	71,944.99	4,858.50	16,726.90	6,610.35	1,68?.68		101,823.42	639.55
	$4,138,354.71	$160,593.51	$1,197,716.35	$251,832.23	$ 61,966.37	$3,901.99	$5,814,365.16	$ 1,604,987.68
July	101,183.67							

Hay permits. $3,784.50, included in Miscellaneous Collections.

INTEREST AND INCOME, STATE UNIVERSITY

Amount expended	$ 85,546.37	
Balance July 1, 1908		$ 8,390.27
Collections		85,293.38
Balance July 1, 1910	8,137.28	
	$ 93,683.65	$ 93,683.65

INTEREST AND INCOME, SCHOOL OF MINES.

Amount expended	$ 34,667.36	
Balance July 1, 1908		$ 3,083.33
Collections		36,260.16
Balance July 1, 1910	4,676.13	
	$ 39,343.49	$ 39,343.49

INTEREST AND INCOME, AGRICULTURAL COLLEGE.

Amount expended	$109,034.05	
Balance July 1, 1908		$ 13,585.16
Collections		128,416.15
Balance July 1, 1910	32,967.26	
	$142,001.31	$142,001.31

INTEREST AND INCOME, VALLEY CITY NORMAL.

Amount expended	$ 47,316.30	
Balance July 1, 1908		$ 3,646.83
Collections		48,615.17
Balance July 1, 1910	4,945.70	
	$ 52,262.00	$ 52,262.00

INTEREST AND INCOME FUND, MAYVILLE NORMAL.

Amount expended	$ 28,787.42	
Balance July 1, 1903		$ 2,331.51
Collections		29,309.80
Balance July 1, 1910	2,853.89	
	$ 31,641.31	$ 31,641.31

INTEREST AND INCOME FUND, BLIND ASYLUM.

Amount expended	$ 25,355.72	
Balance July 1, 1908		$ 2,406.47
Collections		26,521.74
Balance July 1, 1910	3,572.49	
	$ 28,928.21	$ 28,928.21

INTEREST AND INCOME FUND, SCHOOL FOR DEAF AND DUMB.

Amount expended	$ 37,080.26	
Balance July 1, 1908		$ 4,946.00
Collections		35,545.39
Balance July 1, 1910	3,411.13	
	$ 40,491.39	$ 40,491.39

INTEREST AND INCOME FUND, HOSPITAL FOR INSANE.

Amount expended ....:............................. $	8.43	
Balance July 1, 1908 .:.............................		$ 10,494.75
Collections ....:.		17,002.34
Balance July 1, 1910	27,488.66	
	$ 27,497.09	$ 27,497.09

INTEREST AND INCOME FUND, INDUSTRIAL SCHOOL.

Amount expended .... $ 41,534.57		
Balance July 1, 1908		$ 6,255.19
Collections ....•.........		39,438.26
Balance July 1, 1910	4,158.88	
	$ 45,693.45	$ 45,693.45

INTEREST AND INCOME FUND, ACADEMY OF SCIENCE.

Amount expended .... $ 4,456.23		
Balance July 1, 1908		$ 8,589.69
Collections ....•.........................		39,823.50
Balance July 1, 1910	4,056.96	
	$ 48,513.19	$ 48,513.19

INTEREST AND INCOME FUND, REFORM SCHOOL.

Amount expended .... $ 30,004.30		
Balance July 1, 1908 ·............................		$ 14,046.10
Collections		37,875.47
Balance July 1, 1910	21,917.27	
	$ 51,921.57	$ 51,921.57

INTEREST AND INCOME FUND, SOLDIERS' HOME.

Amount expended .... $ 35,134.76		
Balance July 1, 1908		$ 2,426.70
Collections ....•.....		36,939.71
Balance July 1, 1910	4,231.65	
	$ 39,366.41	$ 39,366.41

INTEREST AND INCOME FUND, CAPITOL BUILDING.

Amount expended .... $ 12,126.17		
Balance July 1, 1908 ....·......		$ 46,823.91
Collections		59,160.72
Balance July 1, 1910	93,858.46	
	$105,984.63	$105,984.63

ONE MILL TAX FUND, STATE UNIVERSITY.

Amount expended $166,012.58		
Balance July 1, 1908		$ 847.66
Collections		166,409.37
Balance July 1, 1910	1,244.45	
	$167,257.03	$167,257.03

ONE MILL TAX FUND, AGRICULTURAL COLLEGE.

Amount expended	$100,485.60	
Balance July 1, 1908		$ 510.34
Collections		100,725.72
Balance July 1, 1910	750.46	
	$101,286.06	$101,236.06

ONE MILL TAX FUND, VALLEY CITY NORMAL.

Amount expended	$ 75,273.73	
Balance July 1, 1908		$ 380.36
Collections		75,453.47
Balance July 1, 1910	560.20	
	$ 75,833.83	$ 75,833.83

ONE MILL TAX FUND, MAYVILLE NORMAL.

Amount expended	$ 65,285.42	
Balance July 1, 1908		$ 330.92
Collections		65,441.42
Balance July 1, 1910	486.92	
	$ 65,772.34	$ 65,772.34

ONE MILL TAX FUND, SCHOOL FOR DEAF AND DUMB.

Amount expended	$ 30,357.03	
Balance July 1, 1908		$ 158.70
Collections		30,429.66
Balance July 1, 1910	231.33	
	$ 30,588.36	$ 30,588.36

ONE MILL TAX FUND, SCHOOL OF FORESTRY.

Amount expended	$ 10,078.71	
Balance July 1, 1908		$ 51.83
Collections		10,102.81
Balance July 1, 1910	75.93	
	$ 10,154.64	$ 10,154.64

ONE MILL TAX FUND, INDUSTRIAL SCHOOL.

Amount expended	$ 34,958.63	
Balance July 1, 1908		$ 173.02
Collections		35,042.07
Balance July 1, 1910	256.46	
	$ 35,215.09	$ 35,215.09

ONE MILL TAX FUND, ACADEMY OF SCIENCE.

Amount expended	$ 19,976.36	
Balance July 1, 1908		$ 98.87
Collections		20,024.04
Balance July 1, 1910	146.55	
	$ 20,122.91	$ 20,122.91

STATE BOND SINKING FUND.

Amount expended .... $	.01	
Balance July 1, 1908		$ 32,747.11
Collections		50,326.79
Balance July 1, 1910	83,073.89	

$ 83,073.90 $ 83,073.90

BOND INTEREST FUND.

Amount expended .... $ 59,102.47		
Balance July 1, 1908		$ 37,599.23
Collections		47,437.45
Balance July 1, 1910	25,934.21	

$ 85,036.68 $ 85,036.68

ASYLUM BOND SINKING FUND.

Amount expended .... $	30.01	
Balance July 1, 1908		$ 394.64
Collections		135.76
Balance July 1, 1910	500.39	

$ 530.40 $ 530.40

FINES, PENALTIES AND FORFEITURES.

Amount expended .... $ 29,322.40		
Balance July 1, 1908		$ 1,777.39
Collections		31,765.83
Balance July 1, 1910	4,220.82	

$ 33,543.22 $ 33,543.22

OIL INSPECTION FUND.

Amount expended $100,000.00		
Balance July 1, 1908		$ 49,454.24
Collections		89,418.24
Balance July 1, 1910	38,872.48	

$138,872.48 $138,872.48

SUSPENSE ACCOUNT.

Order No.	Date	To whom issued	Amount
A5338	Nov. 30, 1908	Transfer to Permanent Fund, Academy of Science	$ 584.00

Balance July 1, 1908, ... $ 584.00

ARMORY FUND, NORTH DAKOTA NATIONAL GUARD.

Balance July 1, 1908 .... $ 2,000.00
Transfer to General Fund to credit of Armory Fund N. D.
N. G., Co. "L," Hillsboro.

HOTEL INSPECTION FUND.

Amount expended	$ 5,839.62	
Balance July 1, 1908		$ 289.83
Collections		5,859.00
Balance July 1, 1910	309.21	
	$ 6,148.83	$ 6,148.83

U. S. AID SOLDIERS' HOME.

Amount expended	$ 4,450.00	
Collections		$ 4,450.00
	$ 4,450.00	$ 4,450.00

TWINE PLANT OPERATING FUND.

Overdraft July 1, 1908	$ 135.04	
Amount expended	512,684.02	
Collections		$591,343.72
Balance July 1, 1910	78,524.66	
	$591,343.72	$591,343.72

TWINE PLANT SINKING FUND.

Amount expended	$ 13,520.00	
Balance July 1, 1908		$ 27,647.53
Transfer Twine Operating Fund		11,052.81
Balance July 1, 1910	25,180.34	
	$ 38,700.34	$ 38,700.34

TWINE PLANT CONSTRUCTION FUND.

Balance July 1, 1908		$ 164.91
Balance July 1, 1910	$ 164.91	
	$ 164.91	$ 164.91

WARRANTS WOLF BOUNTY FUND, BIENNIAL PERIOD.

July, 1908	$ 10,599.50
July	*10.17
August	585.00
September	77.50
October	512.50
November	212.50
December	282.00
January, 1909	745.50
February	9,987.50
March	333.00
April	2,699.00
May	5,327.50
June	7,402.50
July	3,957.50
August	995.00
September	4,437.50
October	1,985.50
November	1,694.50
December	1,790.00
January, 1910	1,385.00

February	1,027.50
March	1,650.00
April	1,696.00
May	3,857.50
June	8,112.50
Total	71,362.67
General fund warrants	2,543,567.88
Miscellaneous orders	5,360,264.15

Total cash payments all funds, biennial period $7,975,194.70

COLLECTIONS WOLF BOUNTY FUND, BIENNIAL PERIOD.

July, 1908	$ 699.16
August	
September	553.08
October	12.85
November	2,172.46
December	1,330.72
January, 1909	2,980.80
February	6,200.96
March	7,390.41
April	13,603.52
May	9,100.56
June	1,179.88
July	
August	
September	1,596.27
October	219.33
November	807.04
December	3,386.24
January, 1910	4,018.87
February	6,773.99
March	20,296.80
April	12,679.65
May	5,155.45
June	750.89
Total	$ 100,908.93

Balance July 1, 1908		$ 15,828.67
Collections (tax)		100,908.93
Collections (refund)		47.50
Payments	$ 71,362.67	
Balance July 1, 1910	45,422.43	
	$116,785.10	$116,785.10

*Dishonored Cavalier county draft.

PART TWO

WARRANT ACCOUNT

This part will give collections and payments out of every subdivision of the General Fund, which subdivisions are provided for by appropriations—specific and unlimited—by the Legislative Assembly. Part one takes up every account which is not provided for by either specific or unlimited appropriation by the Legislative Assembly.

GENERAL FUND

MONTH	Balance First of Month	Taxes	COLLECTIONS		Commissioner of Insurance Fees	Clerk Supreme Court Fees	Agriculture and Labor Fees
			Secretary of State				
			Fees	Incorp. Tax			
July, 1908	$ 62,907.89	$ 13, 31. 40	$ 30. 75	$ 1,200.00	$ 4,223.97		
August, 1908	246, 93.97		2,832.25	1,545.00		$ 31.95	$ 86.25
September, 1908	89, 35.18	10, 87. 30	880.50	1,465.00	1, 30.40		37.25
October, 1908	13,440.58	244.39	1,159.50	835.00			
November, 1908	43, 30.51	41,529.87	744.75	1,190.00		79.90	58.75
December, 1908	55,523.69	25, 31.24	702.75	725.00			31.90
January, 1909	23,234.28	56,777.66	795.50	1,655.00			114.50
February, 1909	26,772.27	117,887.49	1, 09.30	3, 00	22,776.82	157.10	
March, 1909	68, 36.65	140,426.44	1,734. 30	3,620.00	49, 33.46		60.30
April, 1909	26,052.76	38,717.10				73.15	39.25
May, 1909	88, 88.81	72,979.53	1,280. 7	2,250.00	16,302. 40		
June, 1909	67, 69.19	22, 47.82	09. 40	1,935.00	13,982.09	324.30	98.40
July, 1909	31, 30.77		3,943. 40	1,815.00	85.85		16.25
August, 1909	63, 89.31		1, 07. 40	1, 00		55.40	
September, 1909	71,878.45	39, 32.55	1,145. 40	1,570.00			
October, 1909	39, 95.11	4, 93.15	984. 40	2,660.00	17,872.59		57.50
November, 1909	39,192.40	15, 42.73	83.25	1, 50	1,521. 40	63. 40	43.25
December, 1909	14, 88.66	64, 47.51	1,532.25	2,640.00	38. 40	38.25	59. 30
January, 1910	17,736.50	76,606. 1					26.00
February, 1910	16,897.18	38, 72.44	1,230.00	1,396.00	57. 40	49.50	26. 40
March, 1910	32,675.13	85,643.28	1,227. 30	2,235.00	1,140. 40	98.40	
April, 1910	38,346.73	240,978.94	1,504.75	1,405.00	43, 38.42	148.40	55. 40
May, 1910	53, 33.96	97, 91.96	1, 71. 40	1,580.00		172.25	13. 40
June, 1910	36, 61.34	14, 32.98	1, 99.25	2, 10		63.75	69. 40
July, 1910	43,254.14						
		$1,919,282.74	$28,686.75	$37,976.00	$173,892.00	$2,2 6.75	$ 1,786. 0

GENERAL FUND—Continued.

MONTH	Land Dep't Fees	Puplic Examiner Fees	COLLECTIONS Interest Public Funds	Hunting Permits	Elevator Licenses	Trolley Fares
July, 1908	$ 2,218.00	$ 1,215.00	$ 2,513.10	.....	$ 67.00	$ 195.40
1908	715.00	60.00	2,627.23	.....	94.00	163.60
September, 1908	446.00	.....	2,446.95	.....	30.00	181.85
1908	517.00	.....	2,169.69	.....	34.00	95.80
1908	.....	30.00	1,712.02	$ 119.10	54.00	156.25
December, 1908	2,789.00	1,65.00	1,532.04	2,819.85	40.00	136.15
January, 1909	2,106.00	120.00	1,861.82	446.60	20.00	212.50
1909	968.00	.....	2,334.35	.....	54.00	718.60
1909	2,135.00	470.00	2,519.69	.....	50.00	1,326.50
April, 1909	.....	00	3,20.69	29.25	10.00	25.85
May, 1909	2,536.00	35.00	4,448.63	.....	34.00	182.90
June, 1909	8,881.50	1,940.00	4,362.01	.....	.....	177.15
July, 1909	3,252.00	285.00	4,626.44	.....	3,786.00	197.05
1909	1,16.50	55.00	5,239.82	.....	10,245.00	.....
1909	1,083.50	.....	4,965.95	.....	4,054.00	292.50
October, 1909	513.00	30.00	4,238.29	.....	88.00	99.15
1909	675.50	1,63.10	3,796.50	.....	378.00	99.80
December, 1909	3,056.00	1,40	3,154.57	.....	94.00	146.70
1910	291.00	.....	2,717.83	.....	64.00	169.85
February, 1910	2,739.25	1,935.00	2,410.18	.....	12.00	164.20
March, 1910	1,884.25	.....	2,584.75	.....	38.00	141.35
April, 1910	1,240.50	1,515.00	4,141.90	.....	22.00	160.75
May, 1910	1,327.00	1,030.00	6,272.98	.....	32.00	.....
June, 1910	3,673.00	90.00	6,600.24	.....	62.00	296.10
	$ 44,163.00	$ 19,518.10	$82,481.67	$3,414.80	$21,752.00	$ 5,342.00

GENERAL — Continued.

MONTH	COLLECTIONS				Total credit	Payments
	...tal or Insane	State ...y	Game and Fish Fund	...ds		
July, 1908	$ 1,627.41	$ 162.30	$......	$ 8,589.82	$3, 63.07	$ 46,455.93
July, 1908	......	......	......	......	......	$3.17
August, 1908	2,91.18	285.52	......	2, 27.51	85, 22.48	76,287.00
Septe...r, 1908	1,042.64	128.59	......	150.75	97, 94.46	94,483.88
..., 1908	2,237.66	183.12	......	8,735.20	31, 61.94	87,92.43
..., 1908	......	88.64	......	1,108.82	91, 51.71	35,988.02
December, 1908	5,887.46	81.20	......	30.39	97, 24.67	74,040.39
January, 1909	1,335.66	1,41.88	......	8,259.86	98, 81.26	71,608.99
..., 1909	4,331.50	787.65	......	548.44	36, 81.80	88,675.15
..., 1909	15.33	17.15	......	165.30	23, 80.98	117,58.22
..., 1909	17,40.05	63.75	......	856.89	48, 83.40	169,944.59
..., 1909	6,166.63	251.67	......	7,218.35	87, 24.17	119,654.98
June, 1909	4,870.71	65.26	......	35.86	49, 85.90	98,825.13
July, 1909	13,26.56	98.51	......	7,892.62	84, 37.34	121,368.08
August, 1909	10,142.91	268.35	......	855.08	95, 61.07	123,202.62
..., 1909	37.29	257.11	5,301.85	1,527.19	23, 11.19	183,716.08
..., 1909	10,087.22	173.54	7,530.25	384.15	89, 85.95	59,193.15
..., 1909	3,528.50	469.48	3,780.35	104,959.24	68, 87.10	154,498.44
..., 1910	397.10	2,803.82	4,534.85	2, 99.29	102, 80.50	84,884.00
..., 1910	9,521.08	622.27	2,400.90	8,656.48	18, 82.62	101,915.44
..., 1910	420.32	631.79	......	35,14.61	92, 45.47	159,870.34
..., 1910	1,062.05	......	......	4,023.47	82, 54.38	114,407.65
April, 1910	8,161.78	23.65	932.30	242.47	82, 57.64	108,803.68
May, 1910	5,925.84	1, 24.60	......	363.03	80, 08.12	94,246.78
June, 1910	731.61	66.01	......	622.65	69, 97.93	155,843.79
	$111,038.49	$ 11,305.86	$4,480.50	$206,527.47	....	$2,543,567.88

*Dishonored ... or county draft.

MAINTENANCE CAPITOL.
Chapter 7, Laws of 1909.

Amount expended	$ 77,979.02	
Balance July 1, 1908		$ 2,898.40
Emergency board		11,000.00
Biennial appropriation		75,000.00
Collections		5,526.20
Balance July 1, 1910	16,445.58	
	$ 94,424.60	$ 94,424.60

PROMOTION IMMIGRATION.

Amount expended	$ 30,770.12	
Balance July 1, 1908		$ 9,416.71
Biennial appropriation		30,000.00
Balance July 1, 1910	8,646.59	
	$ 39,416.71	$ 39,416.71

PROMOTION IRRIGATION.

Amount expended	$ 13,442.86	
Balance July 1, 1908		$ 4,791.49
Biennial appropriation		12,000.00
Collections		750.10
Balance July 1, 1910	4,098.73	
	$ 17,541.59	$ 17,541.59

PUBLIC PRINTING.

Amount expended	$ 80,841.70	
Balance July 1, 1908		$ 33,980.15
Collections		208.00
Biennial appropriation		60,000.00
Balance July 1, 1910	13,346.45	
	$ 94,188.15	$ 94,188.15

INSURANCE PUBLIC BUILDINGS.

Amount expended	$ 36,578.92	
Refunds		$ 155.81
Appropriation to cover		36,423.11
	$ 36,578.92	$ 36,578.92

STATE AID HIGH SCHOOLS.

Amount expended	$ 89,748.88	
Biennial appropriation		$ 90,000.00
Balance July 1, 1908		44,837.57
Balance July 1, 1910	45,088.69	
	$134,837.57	$134,837.57

SALARY GOVERNOR.
$3,000.00 per Year.

John Burke, July 1, 1909, to July 1, 1910	$ 5,750.00	
Balance July 1, 1908		$ 1,500.00

Appropriation, biennial 6,000.00
Balance July 1, 1910 .... 1,750.00

                                                 $ 7,500.00 $ 7,500.00

SALARY LIEUTENANT GOVERNOR.
$1,000.00 per Year.

R. S. Lewis, July 1, 1908, to July 1, 1910......... $ 1,916.59
Balance July 1, 1908 .... $ 500.05
Appropriation, biennial 2,000:00
Balance July 1, 1910 ....   583.46

                                                 $ 2,500.05 $ 2,500.05

SALARY SECRETARY OF STATE.
$2,000.00 per Year.

Alfred Blaisdell, July 1, 1908 to July 1, 1910...... $ 3,999.84
Balance July 1, 1908 .... $ 1,000.12
Appropriation, biennial 4,000.00
Balance July 1, 1910 .... 1,000.28

                                                 $ 5,000.12 $ 5,000.12

SALARY STATE AUDITOR.
$2,000.00 per Year.

H. L. Holmes, July 1, 1908, to Jan. 1, 1909........ $ 1,000.12
D. K. Brightbill, Jan. 1, 1909, to July 1, 1910....   2,999.88
Balance July 1, 1908 .... $ 1,000.12
Appropriation, biennial 4,000.00
Balance July 1, 1910 .... 1,000.12

                                                 $ 5,000.12 $ 5,000.12

SALARY STATE TREASURER.
$2,000.00 per Year.

Albert Peterson, July 1, 1908, to Jan. 1, 1909.... $ 1,000.12
G. L. Bickford, Jan. 1, 1909, to July 1, 1910....   2,833.22
Balance July 1, 1908 .... $ 1,000.12
Appropriation, biennial 4,000.00
Balance July 1, 1910 .... 1,166.78

                                                 $ 5,000.12 $ 5,000.12

SALARY COMMISSIONER OF INSURANCE.
$2,000.00 per Year.

E. C. Cooper, July 1, 1908, to July 1, 1910 ...... $ 3,833.34
Balance July 1, 1908 .... $ 1,000.12
Appropriation, biennial 4,000.00
Balance July 1, 1910 .... 1,166.78

                                                 $ 5,000.12 $ 5,000.12

SALARY ATTORNEY GENERAL.
$2,000.00 per Year.

T. F. McCue, July 1, 1908, to Jan. 1, 1909...... $ 1,000.12
Andrew Miller, Jan. 1, 1909, to July 1, 1910......   2,833.22
Balance July 1, 1908 .... $ 1,000.12

Appropriation, biennial		4,000.00
Balance July 1, 1910	1,166.78	

	$ 5,000.12	$ 5,000.12

SALARY SUPERINTENDENT PUBLIC INSTRUCTION.
$2,000.00 per Year.

W. L. Stockwell, July 1, 1908, to July 1, 1910.. $ 3,833.18		
Balance July 1, 1908		$ 1,000.12
Appropriation, biennial		4,000.00
Balance July 1, 1910	1,166.94	

	$ 5,000.12	$ 5,000.12

SALARY COMMISSIONER OF AGRICULTURE AND LABOR.
$2,000.00 per Year.

W. C. Gilbreath, July 1, 1908, to July 1, 1910.... $ 3,999.97		
Balance July 1, 1908		$ 1,000.09
Appropriation, biennial		4,000.00
Balance July 1, 1910	1,000.12	

	$ 5,000.09	$ 5,000.09

SALARY JUDGES SUPREME COURT.
$10,000.00 per Year.

D. E. Morgan, July 1, 1908, to July 1, 1910....... $ 10,000.07		
Balance July 1, 1908		$ 2,500.19
Appropriation, biennial		10,000.00
Balance July 1, 1910	2,500.12	

	$ 12,500.19	$ 12,500.19

Chas. J. Fisk, July 1, 1908, to July 1, 1910........ $ 9,999.92		
Balance July 1, 1908		$ 2,819.91
Appropriation, biennial		10,000.00
Balance July 1, 1910	2,899.99	

	$ 12,899.91	$ 12,819.91

B. F. Spalding, July 1, 1908, to July 1, 1910...... $ 9,999.92		
Balance July 1, 1908		$ 2,727.89
Appropriation, biennial		10,000.00
Balance July 1, 1910	2,727.97	

	$ 12,727.89	$ 12,727.89

S. E. Ellsworth, Jan. 18, 1909, to July 1, 1910.... $ 7,277.68		
Appropriation, biennial		10,000.00
Balance July 1, 1910	2,722.32	

	$ 10,000.00	$ 10,000.00

John Carmody, Jan. 18, 1909, to July 1, 1910..... $ 7,277.68		
Appropriation, biennial		10,000.00
Balance July 1, 1910	2,722.32	

	$ 10,000.00	$ 10,000.00

SALARY CLERK SUPREME COURT.
$2,000.00 per Year.

R. D. Hoskins, July 1, 1908, to July 1, 1910...... $ 3,583.22		
Balance July 1, 1908		$ 750.00

Appropriation, biennial		4,000.00
Balance July 1, 1910	1,166.78	
	$ 4,750.00	$ 4,750.00

SALARY SUPREME COURT REPORTER.
$1,500.00 per Year.

F. W. Ames, July 1, 1908, to July 1, 1910	$ 3,000.00	
Balance July 1, 1908		$ 1,125.00
Appropriation, biennial		3,000.00
Balance July 1, 1910	1,125.00	
	$ 4,125.00	$ 4,125.00

SALARY STENOGRAPHER SUPREME COURT.
Unlimited.

Ida. M. Fisk	$ 1,875.00
P. L. Keating	1,291.00
E. J. Moore, Jr.	840.00
Walter Devit	675.00
I. Mark Oseth	650.00
Harry Rittgers	632.00
H. D. Bell	337.50
H. C. Bradley	215.00
George Schnepper	177.00
Florence Johnson	150.00
A. I. Stone	140.00
Willotta McGashan	10.00
Inez J. Potter	10.00
Total amount expended	$ 6,852.50

SALARY MARSHAL SUPREME COURT.
$4.00 per day time actually in attendance to court.

Amount expended .... $ 264.00

SALARY ADJUTANT GENERAL.
$1,800.00 per Year.

T. H. Poole, July 1, 1908, to Jan. 7, 1909	$ 935.00	
A. P. Peake, Jan. 8, 1909, to July 1, 1910	2,515.00	
Balance July 1, 1908		$ 900.00
Biennial appropriation		3,600.00
Balance July 1, 1910	1,050.00	
	$ 4,500.00	$ 4,500.00

SALARY JUDGES DISTRICT COURT.
$4,000 per Year.

Chas. Templeton, First District, 24 months	$ 7,416.65
John F. Cowan, Second district, 24 months	7,416.73
Chas. Pollock, Third district, 24 months	7,416.73
Frank P. Allen, Fourth district, 24 months	7,416.73
E. T. Burke, Fifth district, 24 months	7,416.68
W. H. Winchester, Sixth district, 24 months	7,416.71
W. J. Kneeshaw, Seventh district, 24 months	7,416.73
E. B. Goss, Eighth district, 24 months	7,416.68

A. G. Burr, Ninth district, 18 months............   5,665.61
W. C. Crawford, Tenth district, 18 months.......   5,666.61 ·

	$ 70,666.86	
Balance July 1, 1908		$ 14,049.50
Biennial appropriation		80,000.00
Balance July 1, 1910	23,382.64	
	$ 94,049.50	$ 94,049.50

RELIEF OF JUDGE A. G. BURR.
Chapter 36, S. L. 1909.

Salary while acting as District Judge of the Ninth Judicial district for a period of four months.

Amount expended .... $ 1,333.34	
Appropriation	$ 1,333.34

SALARY RAILROAD COMMISSIONERS.
Three Commissioners, $1,200.00 per Year.

C. S. Diesem, July 1, 1908, to Jan. 1, 1909....... $	600.00	
Eric Stafne, July 1, 1908, to Jan. 1, 1909.........	600.00	
Simon Westby, July 1, 1908, to Jan. 1, 1909......	700.00	
W. H. Mann, Jan. 1, 1909, to July 1, 1910........	1,700.00	
O. P. N. Anderson, Jan. 1, 1909, to July 1, 1910..	1,700.00	
W. H. Stutsman, Jan. 1, 1909, to July 1, 1910....	1,700.00	
	$ 7,000.00	
Balance July 1, 1908		$ 1,900.00
Appropriation, biennial		7,200.00
Balance July 1, 1910	2,100.00	
	$ 9,100.00	$ 9,100.00

SALARY SECRETARY RAILROAD COMMISSIONERS.
$2,000.00 per Year.

J. W. Foley, July 1, 1908, to Jan. 1, 1909 .... $	500.06	
Thomas Hall, Jan. 1, 1909, to April 1, 1910	2,499.90	
Balance July 1, 1908		$ 500.06
Appropriation, biennial		4,000.00
Balance July 1, 1910	· 1,500.10	
	$ 4,500.06	$ 4,500.06

TWO PER CENT. INSURANCE PREMIUMS AID FIRE DEPARTMENTS.

Amount expended .... $ 36,837.88	
Appropriation to cover	$ 36,837.88
$ 36,837.88	$ 36,837.88

SALARY DEPUTY OIL INSPECTORS.

Ports of entry.	Amount expended.
Ardock .... $	280.00
Zeeland	210.00
Ellendale	437.50
Fairmount	220.00
Oakes .... ,.....................	230.00

Hettinger	185..00	
Minot ·..............	157.70	
Cogswell	70.00	
Wahpeton ....;...	1,695.00	
Hankinson	2,166.62	
Grand Forks	2,266.62	
Fargo	2,116.62	

Appropriation to cover .... $ 10,035.06

                                  $ 10,035.06 $ 10,035.06

SALARY STATE OIL INSPECTOR.
$2,500.00 per Year.

Frank A. Willson, July 1, 1909, to July 1, 1910.. $ 4,791.66		
Balance July 1, 1908		$ 1,250.05
Appropriation, biennial		5,000.00
Balance July 1, 1910	1,458.39	

                                  $ 6,250.05 $ 6,250.05

SALARY DAIRY COMMISSIONER.
$1,800.00 per Year.

R. F. Flint, July 1, 1909, to July 1, 1910.......... $ 1,650.00		
Appropriation, biennial		$ 3,600.00
Balance July 1, 1910	1,950.00	

                                  $ 3,600.00 $ 3,600.00

SALARY ASSISTANT DAIRY COMMISSIONER.
$1,500.00 per Year.

R. F. Flint, July 1, 1908, to July 1, 1909.......... $ 1,500.00		
E. H. Pierce, July 1, 1909, to July 1, 1910........	1,375.00	
Balance July 1, 1908		$ 750.00
Appropriation, biennial		3,000.00
Balance July 1, 1910	875.00	

                                  $ 3,750.00 $ 3,750.00

SALARY SUPERINTENDENT STATE, BOARD OF HEALTH.
$1,200.00 per Year.

Dr. J. Grassick, July 1, 1908, to July 1, 1910.... $ 2,400.00		
Balance July 1, 1908		$ 900.00
Appropriation, biennial		2,400.00
Balance July 1, 1910	900.00	

                                  $ 3,300.00 $ 3,300.00

SALARY STATE LIBRARIAN.
$1,000.00 per Year.

N. L. Call, July 1, 1908, to July 1, 1910........... $ 1,916.75		
Balance July 1, 1908		$ 500.14
Appropriation, biennial		2,000.00
Balance July 1, 1910	583.39	

                                  $ 2,500.14 $ 2,500.14

SALARY STATE EXAMINER.
$3,000.00 per Year.

Oliver Knudson, July 1, 1908 to July 1, 1910......	$ 5,249.96	
Balance July 1, 1908		$ 1,044.93
Appropriation, biennial		6,000.00
Balance July 1, 1910	1,794.97	
	$ 7,044.93	$ 7,044.93

SALARY DEPUTY STATE EXAMINERS.
Five at $1,800.00 per Year.
One at $1,500.00 per Year.

Jos. M. Fahey, July 1, 1908, to July 1, 1910......	$ 3,325.00	
Roy A. Nelson, Dec. 1, 1908, to July 1, 1910......	2,618.33	
Richard Peyton, July 1, 1908, to July 10, 1909....	1,850.00	
J. F. Hoffmann, April 1, 1909, to July 1, 1910....	2,016.66	
W. J. Dohney, July 1, 1908, to Mar. 8, 1909......	1,240.00	
J. B. Mooney, July 1, 1908, to Dec. 1, 1908......	750.00	
L. J. Bleecker, April 1, 1909, to July 1, 1910......	2,100.00	
Jno. Vallely, April 8, 1909, to July 1, 1910......	2,065.00	
S. H. Wilson, July 10, 1909, to July 1, 1910......	1,333.33	
Balance July 1, 1908		$ 5,351.08
Appropriation, biennial		21,000.00
Balance July 1, 1910	9,052.76	
	$ 26,351.08	$ 26,351.08

PERSONAL EXPENSE. GOVERNOR.
$1,500.00 per Year.

John Burke, July 1, 1908, to July 1, 1910........	$ 2,375.00	
Balance July 1, 1908		$ 250.00
Appropriation, biennial		3,000.00
Balance July 1, 1910	875.00	
	$ 3,250.00	$ 3,250.00

PERSONAL EXPENSE SECRETARY OF STATE.
$750.00 per Year.

Alfred Blaisdell, July 1, 1908, to July 1, 1910....	$ 1,375.00	
Balance July 1, 1908		$ 250.00
Appropriation, biennial		1,500.00
Balance July 1, 1910	375.00	
	$ 1,750.00	$ 1,750.00

PERSONAL EXPENSE, STATE AUDITOR.
$750.00 per Year.

H. L. Holmes, July 1, 1908, to Jan. 1, 1909........	$ 250.00	
D. K. Brightbill, Jan. 1, 1909, to July 1, 1910....	1,062.50	
Balance July 1, 1908		250.00
Appropriation, biennial		1,500.00
Balance July 1, 1910	437.50	
	$ 1,750.00	$ 1,750.00

PERSONAL EXPENSE STATE TREASURER
$750.00 per Year.

Albert Peterson, July 1, 1908, to Jan. 1, 1909.... $	250.00		
G. L. Bickford, Jan. 1, 1909, to July 1, 1910......	1,125.00		
Balance July 1, 1908		$	250.00
Appropriation, biennial			1,500.00
Balance July 1, 1910	375.00		
	$ 1,750.00	$	1,750.00

PERSONAL EXPENSE COMMISSIONER OF INSURANCE.
$750.00 per Year.

E. C. Cooper, July 1, 1908, to July 1, 1910........ $	1,312.50		
Balance July 1, 1908		$	250.00
Appropriation, biennial			1,500.00
Balance July 1, 1910	437.50		
	$ 1,750.00	$	1,750.00

PERSONAL EXPENSE ATTORNEY GENERAL.
$750.00 per Year.

T. F. McCue, July 1, 1908, to Jan. 1, 1909........ $	250.00		
Andrew Miller, Jan. 1, 1909, to July 1, 1910......	1,062.50		
Balance July 1, 1908		$	250.00
Appropriation, biennial			1,500.00
Balance July 1, 1910	437.50		
	$ 1,750.00	$	1,750.00

PERSONAL EXPENSE SUPERINTENDENT OF PUBLIC INSTRUCTION.
$750.00 per Year.

W. L. Stockwell, July 1, 1908, to July 1, 1910.... $	1,312.50		
Balance July 1, 1908		$	250.00
Appropriation, biennial			1,500.00
Balance July 1, 1910	437.50		
	$ 1,750.00	$	1,750.00

PERSONAL EXPENSE COMMISSIONER OF AGRICULTURE AND LABOR.
$750.00 per Year.

W. C. Gilbreath, July 1, 1908, to July 1, 1910.... $	1,375.00		
Balance July 1, 1908		$	250.00
Appropriation, biennial			1,500.00
Balance July 1, 1910	375.00		
	$ 1,750.00	$	1,750.00

PERSONAL EXPENSE CLERK OF SUPREME COURT.

R. D. Hoskins, July 1, 1908, to Jan. 1, 1909...... $	250.00		
Balance July 1, 1908		$	250.00
	$ 250.00	$	250.00

PERSONAL EXPENSE JUDGES SUPREME COURT.
$500.00 per Year Each.

D. E. Morgan, July 1, 1908, to July 1, 1910...... $	875.00	
Chas. J. Fisk, July 1, 1908, to July 1, 1910......	875.00	
B. F. Spalding, July 1, 1908, to July 1, 1910......	875.00	
S. E. Ellsworth, Jan. 18, 1909, to July 1, 1910....	602.89	
John Carmody, Jan. 18, 1909, to July 1, 1910......	602.89	
Balance July 1, 1908		$ 1,070.79
Appropriation, biennial		5,000.00
Balance July 1, 1910	2,240.01	

$ 6,070.79 $ 6,070.79

PERSONAL EXPENSE STATE OIL INSPECTOR.

Frank A. Willson, July 1, 1908, to Jan. 1, 1909.... $	250.00	
Balance July 1, 1908		$ 250.00

$ 250.00 $ 250.00

PERSONAL EXPENSE COMMISSIONER U. AND S. LANDS.

O. I. Hegge, July 1, 1908, to Jan. 1, 1909......... $	250.00	
Balance July 1, 1908		$ 250.00

$ 250.00 $ 250.00

PERSONAL EXPENSE JUDGES DISTRICT COURT.

Chas. Templeton, First district, July 1, 1908, to Jan. 1, 1909 .... $	250.00	
John F. Cowan, Second district, July 1, 1908, to Jan. 1, 1909	250.00	
Chas. A. Pollock, Third district, July 1, 1908, to Jan. 1, 1909	250.00	
Frank P. Allen, Fourth district, July 1, 1908, to Jan. 1, 1909	250.00	
Edward T. Burke, Fifth district, July 1, 1908, to Jan. 1, 1909	250.00	
W. H. Winchester, Sixth district, July 1, 1908, to Jan. 1, 1909	250.00	
W. J. Kneeshaw, Seventh district, July 1, 1908, to Jan. 1, 1909	250.00	
E. B. Goss, Eighth district, July 1, 1908, to Jan. 1, 1909	250.00	
Balance July 1, 1908		$ 2,000.00

$ 2,000.00 $ 2,000.00

PERSONAL EXPENSE ADJUTANT GENERAL.

T. H. Poole, July 1, 1908, to Jan. 1, 1909........ $	250.00	
Balance July 1, 1908		$ 250.00

$ 250.00 $ 250.00

EXPENSE, SUPERINTENDENT STATE BOARD OF HEALTH.
$1,500.00 per Year.

Amount expended from July 1, 1909, to July 1, 1910 $	3,070.03	
Balance July 1, 1908		$ 2,285.58
Appropriation, biennial		3,000.00
Balance July 1, 1910	2,215.55	

$ 5,285.58 $ 5,285.58

EXPENSE, SUPERINTENDENT PUBLIC INSTRUCTION.
$1,000.00 per Year.

Amount expended from July 1, 1908, to July 1, 1910 $ 1,294.69		
Balance July 1, 1908	$	106.07
Appropriation, biennial		2,000.00
Balance July 1, 1910	811.38	
	$ 2,106.07	$ 2,106.07

EXPENSE, CLERK SUPREME COURT.

Amount expended from July 1, 1908, to July 1, 1910 $ 213.29		
Appropriation to cover	$	213.29
	$ 213.29	$ 213.29

CLERKHIRE, GOVERNOR.

Private Secretary .... $2,000.00 per year.		
Clerk .... 1,000.00 per year.		
Amount expended .... $ 5,833.37		
Balance July 1, 1908	$	1,664.99
Appropriation, biennial ....*.......		6,000.00
Balance July 1, 1910	1,831.62	
	$ 7,664.99	$ 7,664.99

CLERKHIRE, SECRETARY OF STATE.

Deputy .... $1,800.00 per year.		
Chief Clerk .... 1,500.00 per year.		
Printing Expert .... 1,500.00 per year.		
Clerk .... 1,200.00 per year.		
Stenographer .... 900.00 per year.		
Stenographer .... 900.00 per year.		
Amount expended .... $ 14,042.68		
Balance July 1, 1908 ....:	$	3,155.00
Appropriation, biennial ....:		7,800.00
Collection to July 1, 1910		655.00
Emergency appropriation		6,782.68
Balance July 1, 1910	4,350.00	
	$ 18,392.68	$ 18,392.68

CLERKHIRE, STATE AUDITOR.

Deputy .... $1,800.00 per year.		
Chief Clerk .... 1,500.00 per year.		
Clerk .... 1,200.00 per year.		
Clerk .... 1,200.00 per year.		
Stenographer .... 900.00 per year.		
Amount expended .... $ 13,504.15		
Balance July 1, 1908 .... $ 2,996.59		
Appropriation, biennial		11,400.00
Emergency appropriation for Board of Equalization 1908 and 1909		841.20
Emergency appropriation		2,591.31
Balance July 1, 1910	4,324.95	
	$ 17,829.10	$ 17,829.10

—3—

CLERKHIRE, STATE TREASURER.

Deputy	$1,800.00 per year.	
Chief Clerk	1,500.00 per year.	
Clerk	1,200.00 per year.	
Stenographer	1,000.00 per year.	

Amount expended	$ 11,200.01	
Balance July 1, 1908		$ 2,737.75
Appropriation, biennial		10,000.00
Emergency appropriation		2,000.00
Balance July 1, 1910	3,537.74	
	$ 14,737.75	$ 14,737.75

CLERKHIRE, COMMISSIONER OF AGRICULTURE AND LABOR.

Deputy	$1,800.00 per year.	
Chief Clerk	1,500.00 per year.	
Stenographer	1,000.00 per year.	

Amount expended	$ 7,841.63	
Balance July 1, 1908		$ 1,950.00
Appropriation, biennial		5,400.00
Emergency appropriation		3,000.00
Balance July 1, 1910	2,508.37	
	$ 10,350.00	$ 10,350.00

CLERKHIRE, SUPERINTENDENT PUBLIC INSTRUCTION.

Deputy	$1,800.00 per year.	
Deputy (Inspector)	1,800.00 per year.	
Stenographer	900.00 per year.	
Clerk	780.00 per year.	

Amount expended	$ 10,422.50	
Balance July 1, 1908		$ 3,107.50
Appropriation, biennial		8,000.00
Emergency appropriation		3,600.00
Balance July 1, 1910	4,285.00	
	$ 14,707.50	$ 14,707.50

CLERKHIRE, COMMISSIONER OF INSURANCE.

Deputy	$1,800.00 per year.	
Chief Clerk	1,200.00 per year.	
Clerk	900.00 per year.	
Stenographer	900.00 per year.	

Amount expended	$ 9,475.00	
Balance July 1, 1908		$ 2,502.50
Appropriation, biennial		7,200.00
Emergency appropriation		2,475.00
Balance July 1, 1910	2,702.50	
	$ 12,177.50	$ 12,177.50

CLERKHIRE, STATE EXAMINER.

Chief Clerk	$1,000.00 per year.	
Stenographer	900.00 per year.	

Amount expended	$ 3,399.84	
Balance July 1, 1908		$ 1,550.07

Appropriation, biennial 2,000.00
Emergency appropriation 900.00
Balance July 1, 1910 .... 1,050.23

$ 4,450.07 $ 4,450.07

CLERKHIRE, SUPREME COURT.
Deputy, $1,500.00 per year.

Amount expended .... $ 2,950.00
Balance July 1, 1908 .... $ 1,301.67
Appropriation, biennial 2,400.00
Balance July 1, 1910 .... 751.67

$ 3,701.67 $ 3,701.67

SALARY, ASSISTANT ATTORNEYS GENERAL.
$2,500.00 per year each.

Alfred Zuger, July 1, 1909, to July 1, 1910........ $ 2,291.64
C. L. Young, July 1, 1909, to July 1, 1910........ 2,291.63
Appropriation, July 1, 1909, to Jan. 1, 1911...... $ 7,500.00
Balance July 1, 1910 .... 2,916.73

$ 7,500.00 $ 7,500.00

SALARY, MEMBER SUPERIOR GRAIN AND WAREHOUSE COMMISSION.
$300.00 per year.

W. C. Macfadden, July 1, 1908, to Feb. 15, 1909... $ 237.50
Jas. E. Kernan, Feb. 16, 1909, to July 1, 1910.... 387.50
Balance July 1, 1908 .... $ 237.50
Appropriation, biennial 600.00
Balance July 1, 1910 .... 212.50

$ 837.50 $ 837.50

CLERKHIRE, RAILROAD COMMISSIONERS.
Stenographer, $720.00 per year.

Amount expended .... $ 848.90
Appropriation, biennial .... $ 1,200.00
Balance July 1, 1910 .... 351.10

$ 1,200.00 $ 1,200.00

CLERKHIRE, ATTORNEY GENERAL.

Assistant's salary charged as clerkhire up to July 1, 1909, thereafter salary, Assistant Attorneys General.
Chapter 219, S. L. 1909, amending Sec. 126, R. C. 1905.

Assistant $1,800.00
Stenographer 900.00
Stenographer 900.00

Amount expended .... $ 4,349.58
Balance July 1, 1908 .... $ 4,101.94
Appropriation, biennial 5,300.00
Balance July 1, 1910 .... 5,052.36

$ 9,401.94 $ 9,401.94

CLERKHIRE AND EXPENSE, ADJUTANT GENERAL.
Clerk, $1,000.00 per year.

Amount expended .... $	1,968.25	
Balance July 1, 1908		$ 605.15
Appropriation, biennial ....\................		2,000.00
Balance July 1, 1910	636.90	
	$ 2,605.15	$ 2,605.15

EXPENSE, STATE EXAMINER.

Amount expended from July 1, 1908, to July 1, 1910 $	1,294.58	
Appropriation to cover	.	$ 1,294.58
	$ 1,294.58	$ 1,294.58

EXPENSE, DEPUTY STATE EXAMINERS.

Amount expended from July 1, 1908, to July 1, 1910. $	8,665.46	
Appropriation to cover ......,....................	.	$ 8,665.46
	$ 8,665.46	$ 8,665.46

LEGAL EXPENSE, ATTORNEY GENERAL.

Amount expended from July 1, 1908, to July 1, 1910 $	4,694.26	
Appropriation to cover		$ 4,694.26
	$ 4,694.26	$ 6,694.26

OFFICE EXPENSE, STATE OIL INSPECTOR.

Amount expended from July 1, 1908, to July 1, 1910 $	2,561.50	
Appropriation to cover		$ 2,561.50
	$ 2,561.50	$ 2,561.50

MILLING STATION, AGRICULTURAL COLLEGE.

Amount expended .... $	2,640.39	
Appropriation (maintenance)		$ 1,000.00
Appropriation, Chap. 116, S. L. 1909		5,000.00
Balance July 1, 1910	3,359.61	
	$ 6,000.00	$ 6,000.00

SCHOOL FOR DEAF (SPUR TRACK ACCOUNT).

Amount expended .... $	329.98	
Balance July 1, 1908		$ 331.00
Balance July 1, 1910	1.02	
	$ 331.00	$ 331.00

SCHOOL FOR DEAF (LAND ACCOUNT).

Balance July 1, 1908		$ 660.00
Balance July 1, 1910 .... $	660.00	
	$ 660.00	$ 660.00

DEFICIENCY AND BUILDING FUND, EDGELEY SUB-STATION.

Balance July 1, 1908		$ 200.00
Balance July 1, 1910 .... $	200.00	
	$ 200.00	$ 200.00

SERUM INSTITUTE, AGRICULTURAL COLLEGE.

Amount expended .... $	2,333.30	
Appropriation		$ 5,333.30
Balance July 1, 1910	3,000.00	
	$ 5,333.30	$ 5,333.30

WILLISTON EXPERIMENTAL STATION.

Amount expended .... $	11,182.97	
Balance July 1, 1908		$ 7,344.33
Appropriation (improvement)		7,000.00
Balance July 1, 1910	3,161.36	
	$ 14,344.33	$ 14,344.33

SCHOOL LAW COMPILATION COMMISSION.

Amount expended .... $	281.26	
Appropriation to cover		$ 281.26
	$ 281.26	$ 281.26

INTEREST ON BONDS.

Amount expended .... $	7,600.00	
Balance July 1, 1908		$ 5,600.00
*Overdraft July 1, 1910		2,000.00
	$ 7,600.00	$ 7,600.00

*Transfer to be made from Bond Interest Fund to cover overdraft.

CRUELTY TO ANIMALS.

Amount expended .... $	453.40	
Appropriation from November 4, 1909 to December 31, 1910		$ 579.18
Balance July 1, 1910	125.78	
	$ 579.18	$ 579.18

CARE SMALLPOX PATIENTS.

Amount expended .... $	15.00	
Appropriation to cover		$ 15.00
	$ 15.00	$ 15.00

BOARD OF GRAIN COMMISSIONERS.

Amount expended ....,..... .... $	4,850.24	
Appropriation		$ 8,450.24
Balance July 1, 1910	3,600.00	
	$ 8,450.24	$ 8,450.24

BOARD OF EXPERTS, PENITENTIARY.

Amount expended	$ 2,187.65	
Appropriation to cover		$ 2,187.65
	$ 2,187.65	$ 2,187.65

EXPENSE ELEVENTH LEGISLATIVE ASSEMBLY.

Amount expended	$ 15,800.54	
Appropriation to cover		$ 15,800.54
	$ 15,800.54	$ 15,800.54

PUBLISHING CONSTITUTIONAL AMENDMENTS.

Amount expended	$ 2,123.00	
Appropriation to cover		$ 2,123.00
	$ 2,123.00	$ 2,123.00

STALLION REGISTRATION BOARD.

Amount expended	$ 88.50	
Appropriation to cover		$ 88.50
	$ 88.50	$ 88.50

ACTIONS AGAINST STATE, JUDGMENTS, COSTS.

Amount expended	$ 211.91	
Appropriation to cover		$ 211.91
	$ 211.91	$ 211.91

EXPENSE TENTH LEGISLATIVE ASSEMBLY.

Amount expended	$ 320.00	
Appropriation to cover		$ 320.00
	$ 320.00	$ 320.00

MILEAGE AND PER DIEM MEMBERS ELEVENTH LEGISLATIVE ASSEMBLY.

Amount expended	$ 49,387.50	
Appropriation to cover		$ 49,387.50
	$ 49,387.50	$ 49,387.50

PER DIEM OFFICERS AND EMPLOYES ELEVENTH LEGISLATIVE ASSEMBLY.

Amount expended	$ 32,311.50	
Appropriation to cover		$ 32,311.50
	$ 32,311.50	$ 32,311.50

CONDUCTING DEMONSTRATION FARMS, AGRICULTURAL COLLEGE.

Amount expended	$ 13,608.25	
Balance July 1, 1908		$ 2,395.75
Appropriation		23,212.50
Balance July 1, 1910	12,000.00	
	$ 25,608.25	$ 25,608.25

DICKINSON EXPERIMENTAL STATION.

Amount expended .... $ 2,466.99
Balance July 1, 1908 .... $ 2,466.99
_____
$ 2,466.99 $ 2,466.99

HETTINGER EXPERIMENTAL STATION.

Amount expended .... $ 1,891.97
Appropriation .... $ 10,000.00
Balance July 1, 1910 .... 8,108.03
_____
$ 10,000.00 $ 10,000.00

FLORENCE CRITTENDEN HOME.

Amount expended .... $ 3,517.74
Appropriation from March 3, 1909, to December
  31, 1910 .... $ 5,475.00
Balance July 1, 1910 .... 1,957.26
_____
$ 5,475.00 $ 5,475.00

PURE SEED FUND, AGRICULTURAL COLLEGE.

Amount expended .... $ 1,875.00
Appropriation .... $ 3,750.00
Balance July 1, 1910 .... 1,875.00
_____
$ 3,750.00 $ 3,750.00

FISH HATCHERY. .

Amount expended .... $ 4,988.13
Appropriation .... $ 5,000.00
Balance July 1, 1910 .... 11.87
_____
$ 5,000.00 $ 5,000.00

SITE FOR SAKAKAWEA STATUE.

Balance July 1, 1908 .... $ 1,500.00
Balance July 1, 1910 .... $ 1,500.00
_____
$ 1,500.00 $ 1,500.00

REFUND HUNTING PERMITS.

Amount expended .... $ 35.25
Collections .... $ 35.25
_____
$ 35.25 $ 35.25

RELIEF OF GEORGE MURRAY.

Amount expended .... $ 470.70
Appropriation .... $ 470.70
_____
$ 470.70 $ 470.70

PRESIDENTIAL ELECTORS.

Amount expended	$	155.80	
Appropriation to cover			$ 155.80

	$	155.80	$ 155.80

LIST NEW TAXABLE LANDS.

Amount expended	$	2,146.78	
Appropriation to cover			$ 2,146.78

	$	2,146.78	$ 2,146.78

STATE TREASURER'S BOND PREMIUM.

Amount expended	$	2,280.00	
Appropriation to cover			$ 2,280.00

	$	2,280.00	$ 2,280.00

HONOR AND SERVICE MEDALS, STATE MILITIA.

Balance July 1, 1908			$ 5.50
Balance July 1, 1910	$	5.50	

	$	5.50	$ 5.50

BURIAL DECEASED SOLDIERS.

Amount expended	$	400.00	
Appropriation to cover			$ 400.00

	$	400.00	$ 400.00

BURIAL DECEASED CONVICTS.

Amount expended	$	484.20	
Appropriation to cover			$ 484.20

	$	484.20	$ 484.20

ERECTION HEADSTONE, DECEASED SOLDIERS.

Amount expended	$	80.00	
Appropriation to cover			$ 80.00

	$	80.00	$ 80.00

INTEREST ON PUBLIC FUNDS.

Amount expended	$	13.40	
Appropriation to cover			$ 13.40

	$	13.40	$ 13.40

STATE· FAIR GRAND FORKS AND FARGO.

Amount expended Grand Forks	$	10,000.00	
Amount expended Fargo		10,000.00	
Balance July 1, 1908, Fargo			$ 5,000.00
Appropriation Grand Forks			10,000.00
Appropriation Fargo			10,000.00
Balance July 1, 1910, Fargo............		5,000.00	

	$	25,000.00	$ 25,000.00

ENFORCEMENT PURE FOOD LAW.

Amount expended	$ 13,273.60	
Balance July 1, 1908		$ 3,273.60
Appropriation, biennial		20,000.00
Balance July 1, 1910	10,000.00	
	$ 23,273.60	$ 23,273.60

PRINTING REVISED CODES, 1905.

Balance July 1, 1908		$ 500.00
Unexpended balance cancelled (Sec. 1280, R. C. 1905)	$ 500.00	
	$ 500.00	$ 500.00

ARREST AND RETURN FUGITIVES FROM JUSTICE.

Amount expended	$ 3,343.32	
Appropriation to cover		$ 3,343.32
	$ 3,343.32	$ 3,343.32

REWARD ARREST AND CONVICTION OF HORSE THIEVES.

Amount expended	$ 1,000.00	
Appropriation to cover		$ 1,000.00
	$ 1,000.00	$ 1,000.00

EXPENSE BOARD OF PARDONS.

Amount expended from July 1, 1908, to July 1, 1910	$ 544.85	
Balance July 1, 1908		$ 944.16
Appropriation biennial		1,200.00
Balance July 1, 1910	1,649.31	
	$ 2,194.16	$ 2,194.16

BUILDING FUND, BIOLOGICAL STATION AT DEVILS LAKE.

Amount expended	$ 1,500.00	
Appropriation		$ 5,000.00
Balance July 1, 1910	3,500.00	
	$ 5,000.00	$ 5,000.00

MAINTENANCE BIOLOGICAL STATION AT DEVILS LAKE.

Amount expended	$ 2,092.56	
Appropriation from July 1, 1909 to January 1, 1911		$ 4,500.00
Balance July 1, 1910	2,407.44	
	$ 4,500.00	$ 4,500.00

STATE TUBERCULOSIS SANITARIUM.

Amount expended	$ 3,423.18	
Appropriation		$ 10,000.00
Balance July 1, 1910	6,576.82	
	$ 10,000.00	$ 10,000.00

OFFICE EXPENSE RAILROAD COMMISSIONERS.

Overdraft July 1, 1908 .... $	5.17	
Amount expended from July 1, 1908 to July 1, 1910	1,183.89	
Appropriation		$ 1,000.00
Transferred from traveling expenses railroad commissioners emergency board		400.00
Balance July 1, 1910	210.94	
	$ 1,400.00	$ 1,400.00

STATE LAW LIBRARY.

Amount expended .... $	2,746.46	
Balance July 1, 1908		$ 175.41
Approriation, biennial ......:.....		4,000.00
Balance July 1, 1910	1,428.95	
	$ 4,175.41	$ 4,175.41

RELIEF OF T. R. SHAW, SALARY SECRETARY CAPITOL COMMISSION.

Amount expended .... $	391.20	
Appropriation		$ 391.20
	$ 391.20	$ 391.20

NORTH DAKOTA HISTORICAL SOCIETY.

Amount expended ....: .... $	8,273.86	
Balance July 1, 1908		$ 1,938.82
Appropriation ....•........		9,200.00
Balance July 1, 1910	2,964.96	
	$ 11,138.82	$ 11,138.82

MAINTENANCE SUB-EXPERIMENTAL STATIONS, DICKINSON, LANGDON AND WILLISTON.

Amount expended .... $	12,333.16	
Appropriation to January 1, 1911		$ 27,333.16
Balance July 1, 1910	15,000.00	
	$ 27,333.16	$ 27,333.16

'REIMBURSING PROF. LADD, EXPENSE FLOUR CASE.

Amount expended .... $	2,171.23●.	
Appropriation		$ 2,171.23
	$ 2,171.23	$ 2,171.23

ST. LOUIS EXPOSITION DEFICIT.

Amount expended .... $	155.26	
Appropriation		$ 155.26
	$ 155.26	$ 155.26

CONTINGENCY FUND, GOVERNOR.

Amount expended .... $	405.65	
Balance July 1, 1908		$ 477.10

Appropriation to make $500 annually		290.15
Balance July 1, 1910	361.60	
	$ 767.25	$ 767.25

FLAGS, PUBLIC BUILDINGS.

Amount expended .... $	159.74	
Appropriation to cover ....·		$ 159.74
	$ 159.74	$ 159.74

TRANSPORTATION PATIENTS, HOSPITAL FOR INSANE.

Amount expended	$ 23,528.55	
Appropriation to cover		$ 23,528.55
	$ 23,528.55	$ 23,528.55

TRANSPORTATION CONVICTS, STATE PENITENTIARY.

Amount expended	$ 9,812.45	
Appropriation to cover		$ 9,812.45
	$ 9,812.45	$ 9,812.45

TRANSPORTATION CONVICTS, REFORM SCHOOL.

Amount expended	$ 2,198.54	
Appropriation to cover		$ 2,198.54
	$ 2,198.54	$ 2,198.54

EXPENSE BOARD OF MANAGEMENT STATE NORMAL SCHOOLS

Amount expended .... $	819.24	
Appropriation to cover		$ 819.24
	$ 819.24	$ 819.24

EXPENSE, BOARD OF MANAGEMENT MAYVILLE NORMAL SCHOOL.

Amount expended .... $	862.32	
Appropriation to cover		$ 862.32
	$ 862.32	$ 862.32

EXPENSE, BOARD OF MANAGEMENT VALLEY CITY NORMAL SCHOOL.

Amount expended .... $	619.35	
Appropriation to cover		·$ 619.35
	$ 619.35	$ 619.35

PER DIEM AND EXPENSE, TRUSTEES STATE UNIVERSITY.

Amount expended	$ 1,462.00	
Appropriation to cover		$ 1,462.00
	$ 1,462.00	$ 1,462.00

PER DIEM AND EXPENSE TRUSTEES AGRICULTURAL COLLEGE.

Amount expended .... $ 3,094.70
Appropriation to cover .... $ 3,094.70

                                          $ 3,094.70 $ 3,094.70

PER DIEM AND EXPENSE, TRUSTEES INDUSTRIAL SCHOOL.

Amount expended .... $ 435.40
Appropriation to cover .... $ 435.40

                                          $ 435.40 $ 435.40

PER DIEM AND EXPENSE, TRUSTEES SCIENTIFIC SCHOOL.

Amount expended .... $ 791.95
Appropriation to cover .... $ 791.95

                                          $ 791.95 $ 791.95

PER DIEM AND EXPENSE, TRUSTEES SCHOOL OF FORESTRY.

Amount expended .... $ 561.20
Appropriation to cover .... $ 561.20

                                          $ 561.20 $ 561.20

PER DIEM AND EXPENSE, TRUSTEES SCHOOL FOR DEAF AND DUMB.

Amount expended .... $ 899.30
Appropriation to cover .... $ 899.30

                                          $ 899.30 $ 899.30

PER DIEM AND EXPENSE, TRUSTEES STATE PENITENTIARY.

Amount expended .... $ 2,872.50
Appropriation to cover .... $ 2,872.50

                                          $ 2,872.50 $ 2,872.50

• PER DIEM AND EXPENSE, TRUSTEES REFORM SCHOOL.

Amount expended .... $ 2,239.38
Appropriation to cover .... $ 2,239.38

                                          $ 2,239.38 $ 2,239.38

PER DIEM AND EXPENSE, TRUSTEES HOSPITAL FOR INSANE.

Amount expended .... $ 885.55
Appropriation to cover .... $ 885.55

                                          $ 885.55 $ 885.55

PER DIEM AND EXPENSE, TRUSTEES INSTITUTION FOR FEEBLE MINDED.

Amount expended .... $ 991.10
Appropriation to cover .... $ 991.10

                                          $ 991.10 $ 991.10

PER DIEM AND EXPENSE, TRUSTEES BLIND ASYLUM.

Amount expended	$ 668.90		
Appropriation to cover		$	668.90
	$ 668.90	$	668.90

PER DIEM AND EXPENSE, TRUSTEES SOLDIERS' HOME.

Amount expended	$ 436.20		
Appropriation to cover		$	436.20
	$ 436.20	$·	436.20

EXPENSE SUPREME COURT.

Amount expended from July 1, 1908 to July 1, 1910	$ 2,605.52		
Appropriation to cover		$	2,605.52
	$ 2,605.52	$	2,605.52

PURE PAINT LAW LITIGATION.

Amount expended	$ 1,981.95		
Appropriation to cover			1,981.95
	$ 1,981.95	$	1,981.95

FORT ABERCROMBIE STATE PARK.

Amount expended	$ 214.25		
Appropriation		$	500.00
Balance July 1, 1910	285.75		
	$ 500.00	$	500.00

SALARY, CONDUCTOR TEACHERS' INSTITUTES.

$50.00 annually for each organized county in the state.

Amount expended from July 1, 1908 to July 1, 1910	$ 4,280.00		
Appropriation to cover		$	4,280.00
	$ 4,280.00	$	4,280.00

BOARD OF VETERINARY MEDICAL EXAMINERS.

Amount expended from July 1, 1908 to July 1, 1910	$ 294.05		
Balance July 1, 1908		$	292.39
Collections			890.00
Balance July 1, 1910	888.34		
	$ 1,182.39	$	1,182.39

LIVE STOCK ASSOCIATION.

Amount expended	$ 811.00		
Balance July 1, 1908		$	750.00
Appropriation biennial			1,000.00
Balance July 1, 1910	939.00		
	$ 1,750.00	$	1,750.00

RELIEF OF F. M. BAKER.

Amount expended	$ 450.00	
Appropriation		$ 450.00
	$ 450.00	$ 450.00

MAINTENANCE AND BUILDING FUND, PUBLIC HEALTH LABORATORY, STATE UNIVERSITY.

Amount expended	$ 10,000.00	
Balance July 1, 1908		$ 5,000.00
Appropriation		10,000.00
Balance July 1, 1910	5,000.00	
	$ 15,000.00	$ 15,000.00

BUILDING FUND, HOSPITAL FOR INSANE.

Amount expended	$102,242.49	
Balance July 1, 1908		$ 70,772.91
Appropriation		126,050.00
Balance July 1, 1910	94,580.42	
	$196,822.91	$196,822.91

GAME AND FISH BOARD OF CONTROL.

Amount expended	$ 20,561.03	
Collections		$ 24,480.50
Balance July 1, 1910	3,919.47	
	$ 24,480.50	$ 24,480.50

INDEMNITY DESTRUCTION GLANDERED HORSES.

Amount expended	$ 81,687.33	
Appropriation		$ 80,000.00
Overdraft July 1, 1910		1,687.33
	$ 81,687.33	$ 81,687.33

STATE LIBRARY COMMISSION.

Amount expended	$ 12,376.77	
Balance July 1, 1908		$ 3,296.61
Appropriation		15,600.00
Collections (books missing)		5.10
Balance July 1, 1910	6,524.94	
	$ 18,901.71	$ 18,901.71

LIVE STOCK SANITARY BOARD.

Amount expended	$ 22,739.32	
Balance July 1, 1908		$ 1,737.17
Appropriation		26,000.00
Transferred from Chief Veterinarian expense acct.		856.20
Balance July 1, 1910	5,854.05	
	$ 28,593.37	$ 28,593.37

BUILDING FUND BLIND ASYLUM.

Amount expended	$ 28,042.50	
Balance July 1, 1908		$ 1,358.27
Appropriation		31,000.00
Collections		23.05
Balance July 1, 1910	4,338.82	
	$ 32,381.32	$ 32,381.32

MAINTENANCE AND BUILDING FUND, REFORM SCHOOL.

Amount expended	$ 17,030.85	
Balance July 1, 1908		$ 10,009.74
Appropriation		16,850.00
Collections		190.00
Refund warrant No. 81868		6.00
Balance July 1, 1910	10,024.89	
	$ 27,055.74	$ 27,055.74

MAINTENANCE AND BUILDING FUND, STATE PENITENTIARY.

Amount expended	$186,991.90	
Balance July 1, 1908		$ 83,993.81
Appropriation		150,600.00
Collections		11,305.86
Balance July 1, 1910	58,907.77	
	$245,899.67	$245,899.67

FEES, SELECTING UNIVERSITY AND SCHOOL LANDS.

Amount expended	$ 147.90	
Balance July 1, 1908		$ 188.90
Balance transferred to expense selection indemnity lands	41.00	
	$ 188.90	$ 188.90

EXPENSE SELECTING INDEMNITY LANDS.

Overdraft July 1, 1908	$ 43.54	
Amount expended	13.50	
Transferred from fees, selecting U. and S. lands..		$ 41.00
Transferred from expense, board U. & S. lands...		16.04
	$ 57.04	$ 57.04

EXPENSE APPRAISEMENT AND SALE UNIVERSITY AND SCHOOL LANDS.

Overdraft July 1, 1908	$ 131.29	
Amount expended	11,542.89	
Appropriation, biennial		$ 8,000.00
Collections		130.14
Transferred from expense Board U. & S. Lands...		4,000.00
Balance July 1, 1910	455.96	
	$ 12,130.14	$ 12,130.14

FIRE LOSS STATE UNIVERSITY.

Amount expended .... $	55.00	
Collections		$ 55.00
	$ 55.00	$ 55.00

REFUND ELEVATOR LICENSES.

Amount expended ....•. $	80.00	
Collection		$ 80.00
	$ 80.00	$ 80.00

SALARY TEACHERS IN UNORGANIZED COUNTIES.

Amount expended .... $	80.51	
Balance July 1, 1908		$ 513.90
Balance July 1, 1910 ....,.....	433.39	
	$ 513.90	$ 513.90

STATE HISTORICAL SOCIETY.

Collections		$ 177.00
Balance July 1, 1910 .... $	177.00	
	$ 177.00	$ 177.00

WHITE STONE HILLS BATTLEFIELD COMMISSION.

Amount expended .... $	4,494.87	
Balance July 1, 1908		$ 74.40
Collections		4,423.75
Balance July 1, 1910	3.28	
	$ 4,498.15	$ 4,498.15

ARMORIES FOR NATIONAL GUARD.

Amount expended .... $	20,170.00	
Balance July 1, 1908		$ 10,170.00
Appropriation biennial	•	20,000.00
Balance July 1, 1910	10,000.00	
	$ 30,170.00	$ 30,170.00

STATE POULTRY ASSOCIATION.

Amount expended .... $	600.00	
Balance July 1, 1908		$ 300.00
Appropriation biennial		600.00
Balance July 1, 1910	300.00	
	$ 900.00	$ 900.00

FIRE LOSS AGRICULTURAL COLLEGE.

Collections		$ 40,265.23
Balance July 1, 1910 .... $	40,265.23	
	$ 40,265.23	$ 40,265.23

BUILDING FUND, AGRICULTURAL COLLEGE.

Amount expended	$116,488.92	
Balance July 1, 1908		$ 17,803.25
Appropriation		130,000.00
Balance July 1, 1910	31,314.33	
	$147,803.25	$147,803.25

MAINTENANCE, EDGELEY EXPERIMENTAL STATION.

Amount expended	$ 12,772.80	
Balance July 1, 1908		$ 3,534.15
Appropriation (maintenance)		10,000.00
Appropriation (improvement)		2,500.00
Balance July 1, 1910	3,261.35	
	$ 16,034.15	$ 16,034.15

BUILDING FUND, STATE UNIVERSITY.

Amount expended	$109,085.79	
Balance July 1, 1908		$ 501.55
Appropriation		181,000.00
Balance July 1, 1910	72,415.76	
	$181,501.55	$181,501.55

BUILDING FUND, SCIENTIFIC SCHOOL.

Amount expended	$ 58,693.74	
Balance July 1, 1908		$ 30.23
Appropriation		59,700.00
Balance July 1, 1910	1,036.49	
	$ 59,730.23	$ 59,730.23

MAINTENANCE FUND, SCIENTIFIC SCHOOL.

Overdraft July 1, 1908	$ 4,997.84	
Amount expended	2,163.67	
Collections		$ 5,530.14
Overdraft July 1, 1910		1,631.37
	$ 7,161.51	$ 7,161.51

EXPENSE, BOARD OF UNIVERSITY AND SCHOOL LANDS.

Amount expended	$ 36,415.71	
Balance July 1, 1908		$ 25,327.33
Appropriation, biennial		10,000.00
Collections		44,163.00
Transferred to appropriation and sale University and School Lands	4,000.00	
Transferred to expense selection indemnity lands ..	16.04	
Balance July 1, 1910	39,058.58	
	$ 79,490.33	$ 79,490.33

ADVERTISING AND EXPENSE, LEASING UNIVERSITY AND SCHOOL LANDS.

Amount expended	$ 2,681.63	
Balance July 1, 1908		$ 4,643.63

—4—

Appropriation, biennial 4,000.00
Balance July 1, 1910 ....   5,962.00

                                                          $ 8,643.63 $ 8,643.63

NORTH DAKOTA AID FIREMEN'S ASSOCIATION.

Overdraft July 1, 1908 .... $ 500.00
Amount expended ....•. 3,000.00
Appropriation .... $ 3,000.00
Refund warrant No. 75144 ....   500.00

                                                          $ 3,500.00 $ 3,500.00

GEOLOGICAL SURVEY, AGRICULTURAL COLLEGE.

Amount expended .... $ 1,000.00
Appropriation, biennial .... $ 2,000.00
Balance July 1, 1910 ....   1,000.00

                                                          $ 2,000.00 $ 2,000.00

GEOLOGICAL SURVEY, STATE UNIVERSITY.

Amount expended .... $ 2,000.00
Balance July 1, 1908 .... $ 1,000.00
Appropriation, biennial 2,000.00
Balance July 1, 1910 ....   1,000.00

                                                          $ 3,000.00 $ 3,000.00

SCHOOL OF FORESTRY (COLLECTION ACCOUNT).

Balance July 1, 1908 .... $ 256.24
Collections 1,055.77
Balance July 1, 1910 .... $ 1,312.01

                                                          $ 1,312.01 $ 1,312.01

MAINTENANCE AND BUILDING FUND, INDUSTRIAL SCHOOL.

Overdraft July 1, 1908 .... $ 8,141.21
Amount expended 34,202.69
Appropriation .... $ 36,500.00
Collections 4,167.68
Refund warrant No. 72641 and 73832 ....   8,566.92
Balance July 1, 1910 ....   6,890.70

                                                          $ 49,234.60 $ 49,234.60

MILITARY FUND, INDUSTRIAL SCHOOL.

Amount expended .... $ 37.52
Appropriation .... $ 225.00
Balance July 1, 1910 ....   187.48

                                                          $ 225.00 $ 225.00

LECTURERS, TEACHERS INSTITUTES.

Amount expended from July 1, 1908, to July 1, 1910 $ 1,829.76
Appropriation to cover .... $ 1,829.76

                                                          $ 1,829.76 $ 1,829.76

JURISDICTION OVER UNORGANIZED COUNTIES.

Amount expended .... $ 3,375.10

STATE DIPPING TANKS.

Amount expended from July 1, 1908, to July 1, 1910 $	37.50	
Balance July 1, 1908		$ 2,809.29
Collections (fees)		100.00
Balance July 1, 1910	2,871.79	
	$ 2,909.29	$ 2,909.29

EXPENSE, FARMERS INSTITUTES.

Amount expended from July 1, 1908, to July 1, 1910 $ 20,787.40		
Balance July 1, 1908		$ 9,582.72
Appropriation		• 12,000.00
Collections		6.80
Balance July 1, 1910	801.62	
	$ 21,589.02	$ 21,589.02

MILEAGE AND PER DIEM, MEMBERS LIVE STOCK SANITARY BOARD.

Amount expended .... $	747.55	
Refund warrant No. 72775		$ .50
Appropriation to cover		747.05
	$ 747.55	$ 747.55

LANGDON EXPERIMENTAL STATION.

Amount expended .... $ 10,000.00		
Balance July 1, 1908		$ 10,000.00
	$ 10,000.00	$ 10,000.00

PUBLIC SERVICE INQUIRY COMMISSION.

Amount expended .... $	6.20	
Appropriation to cover		$ 6.20
	$ 6.20	$ 6.20

TRAVELING EXPENSE RAILROAD COMMISSIONERS.
$200.00 per year each.

Amount expended from July 1, 1908, to July 1, 1910 $	1,385.85	
Balance July 1, 1908		$ 456.27
Appropriation, biennial, $1,600.00, less $400.00 transferred to office expense, Railroad Commissioners Emergency Board		1,200.00
Balance July 1, 1910 ....,...............	270.42	
	$ 1,656.27	$ 1,656.27

EXPENSE, DAIRY COMMISSIONER.

Amount expended from July 1, 1908, to July 1, 1910 $	3,102.75	
Balance July 1, 1908		$ 3,982.09
Appropriation		2,500.00
Collections (licenses)		2,790.00
Balance July 1, 1910	4,169.34	
	$ 7,272.09	$ 7,272.09

TRAVELING EXPENSE, STATE OIL INSPECTOR.

Amount expended from July 1, 1908, to July 1, 1910 $	989.93	
Appropriation to cover		$ 989.93
	$ 989.93	$ 989.93

EXPENSE, CHIEF VETERINARIAN.

Balance July 1, 1908	$ 856.20
Transferred to credit of Live Stock Sanitary Board.	

EXPENSE, STATE MILITIA.

Amount expended from July 1, 1908, to July 1, 1910 $	43,497.94	
Balance July 1, 1908		$ 15,542.10
Appropriation, biennial		45,400.00
Collections		53.06
Balance July 1, 1910	17,497.22	
	$ 60,995.16	$ 60,995.16

ROCK ISLAND MILITARY RESERVATION.

Amount expended .... $	1,420.38	
Appropriation		$ 5,000.00
Balance July 1, 1910	3,579.62	
	$ 5,000.00	$ 5,000.00

SCHOOL FOR DEAF (COLLECTION ACCOUNT).

Balance July 1, 1908		$ 421.41
Collections		1,551.39
Balance July 1, 1910 .... $	1,972.80	
	$ 1,972.80	$ 1,972.80

BUILDING FUND, SCHOOL FOR DEAF.

Amount expended .... $	25,400.00	
Appropriation		$ 25,000.00
Overdraft July 1, 1910		400.00
	$ 25,400.00	$ 25,400.00

BUILDING FUND, MAYVILLE NORMAL SCHOOL.

Amount expended	$ 65,719.74	
Balance July 1, 1908		$ 8,387.57
Appropriation		55,500.00
Collections		2,276.06
Balance July 1, 1910	443.89	
	$ 66,163.63	$ 66,163.63

MAINTENANCE AND BUILDING FUND, VALLEY CITY NORMAL SCHOOL.

Amount expended	$ 89,127.03	
Balance July 1, 1908		$ 4,971.15
Appropriation		133,875.00
Balance July 1, 1910	49,719.12	
	$138,846.15	$138,846.15

MAINTENANCE, INSTITUTION FOR FEEBLE MINDED.

Amount expended	$ 94,449.89	
Balance July 1, 1908		$ 19,219.32
Appropriation		73,750.00
Collections		25,469.05
Balance July 1, 1910	33,988.48	
	$128,438.37	$128,438.37

BUILDING FUND, SCHOOL OF FORESTRY.

Amount expended	$ 16,510.15	
Balance July 1, 1908		$ 3,641.27
Appropriation		20,000.00
Balance July 1, 1910	7,131.12	
	$ 23,641.27	$ 23,641.27

PERSONAL EXPENSE RAILROAD COMMISSIONERS.

Amount expended:		
O. P. N. Anderson	$ 499.99	
W. H. Mann	499.99	
W. H. Stutsman	499.99	
Biennial appropriation		$ 2,400.00
Balance July 1, 1910	900.03	
	$ 2,400.00	$ 2,400.00

MAINTENANCE HOSPITAL FOR INSANE.

Amount expended $240,203.88

RECAPITULATION.

Showing total amount of warrants issued account of expense of fund named. July 1, 1908, to July 1, 1910.

Maintenance capitol	$ 77,979.
Promotion immigration	30,770.
Promotion irrigation	13,442.
Public printing	80,841.
Insurance public buildings	36,578.02
State aid high schools	89,748.88
Two per cent. insurance premiums aid fire departments	36, 7.
Salary Governor	5,7
Salary Lieutenant Governor	1 83
Salary Secretary of State	5,950.
Salary State Auditor	4,000.
Salary State Treasurer	3, 3.
Salary Commissioner of Insurance	3,833.
Salary Attorney General	3,
Salary Superintendent Public Instruction	3
Salary Commissioner of Agriculture and Labor	3,888.
Salary Judge Supreme Court	10,000.
Salary Judge Supreme Court	9,999.
Salary Judge Supreme Court	9,999.
Salary Judge Supreme Court	7,277.
Salary Judge Supreme Court	7,277.
Salary Clerk Supreme Court	3, .
Salary Supreme Court Reporter	3,
Salary Stenographer Supreme Court	6, .
Salary Marshal Supreme Court	.
Salary Adjutant General	3,
Salary Judges District Court	70, .88
Relief of Judge A. G. Burr	1,583.88
Salary Railroad Commissioners	7,666.
Salary Secretary Railroad Commissioners	2,999.
Salary Deputy Oil Inspector, Ardock	280.
Salary Deputy Oil Inspector, Zeeland	210.00
Salary Deputy Oil Inspector, Ellendale	437.66
Salary Deputy Oil Inspector, Fairmount	220.00
Salary Deputy Oil Inspector, Oakes	230.00
Salary Deputy Oil Inspector, Hettinger	185.00
Salary Deputy Oil Inspector, Minot	157.70
Salary Deputy Oil Inspector, Cogswell	70.00
Salary Deputy Oil Inspector, Wahpeton	1,695.00
Salary Deputy Oil Inspector, Hankinson	2,166.62
Salary Deputy Oil Inspector, Grand Forks	2,266.62
Salary Deputy Oil Inspector, Fargo	2,116.62
Salary State Oil Inspector	4,791.66
Salary Dairy Commissioner	1,650.00
Salary Assistant Dairy Commissioner	2,875.00
Salary Superintendent State Board of Health	2,400.00
Salary State Librarian	1,916.75
Salary State Examiner	5,249.96
Salary Deputy State Examiners	17,298.32
Personal expense Governor	2,375.00
Personal expense Secretary of State	1,375.00
Personal expense State Auditor	1,312.50
Personal expense State Treasurer	1,375.00
Personal expense Commissioner of Insurance	1,312.50

Personal expense Attorney General ....   1, 1 .
Personal expense Supt. Public Instruction ......   1, 1 .
Personal expense Comm'r Agriculture and Labor   1., 7
Personal expense Clerk Supreme Court ....
Personal expense Judges Supreme Court   3,
Personal expense State Oil Inspector   2
Personal expense Commissioner U. and S. Lands   5⁵.
Personal expense Judges District Court ....   · 2   .
Personal expense Adjutant General ....   50.
Expense Supt. State Board of Health ....   3 0.
Expense Supt. Public Instruction 1,3 4.50
Expense Clerk Supreme Court ....   ,303.00
Clerkhire Governor 5,833.37
Clerkhire Secretary of State 14,042.68
Clerkhire State Auditor 13,504.15
Clerkhire State Treasurer 11,200.01
Clerkhire Comm'r Agriculture and Labor 7,841.63
Clerkhire Superintendent Public Instruction 10,422.50
Clerkhire Commissioner of Insurance 9,475.00
Clerkhire State Examiner 3,399.84
Clerkhire Supreme Court 2,950.00
Salary Assistant Attorneys General ....≈..   4,583.27
Salary Member Superior Grain and Warehouse
  Commission 625.00
Clerkhire Railroad Commissioners 848.90
Clerkhire Attorney General 4,349.58
Clerkhire Adjutant General 1,968.25
Expense State Examiner 1,294.58
Expense Deputy State Examiners 8,665.46
Legal Expense Attorney General 4,694.26
Office expense State Oil Inspector 2,561.50
Milling Station, Agricultural College 2,640.39
School for Deaf (Spur Track account) 329.98
Serum Institute, Agricultural College 2,333.30
Williston Experimental Station 11,182.97
School Law Compilation Commission 281.26
Interest on bonds 7,600.00
Cruelty to animals 453.40
Care small-pox patients 15.00
Board of Grain Commissioners 4,850.24
Board of Experts Penitentiary 2,187.65
Expense Eleventh Legislative Assembly 15,800.54
Publishing Constitutional Amendments 2,123.00
Stallion Registration Board 88.50
Actions against the state, judgments, costs......   211.91
Expense Tenth Legislative Assembly 320.00
Mileage and per diem, members Eleventh Legis-
  lative Assembly 49,387.50
Per diem, officers and employees, Eleventh Leg-
  islative Assembly 32,311.50
Conducting demonstration farms, Agricultural
  College 13,608.25
Dickinson Experimental Station .....·..........   2,466.99
Hettinger Experimental Station 1,891.97
Florence Crittenden Home 3,517.74
Pure Seed Fund, Agricultural College..........   1,875.00
Fish hatchery 4,988.13
Refund hunting permits 35.25
Relief of George Murray 470.70
Presidential electors 155.80

List new taxable lands 2,146.78
State Treasurer's bond premium 2,280.00
Burial deceased soldiers 400.00
Burial deceased convicts 484.20
Erection headstone deceased soldiers 80.00
Interest on public funds 13.40
State fair, Grand Forks and Fargo............. ,000.00
Enforcement pure food law .... ,273.60
Arrest and return fugitives from justice 20,   .32.
Reward arrest and conviction horse thieves...... 13,   .00
Expense board of pardons 343.85
Building fund, Biological Station .... ,644.00
Maintenance, Biological Station .... ,092.56
State Tuberculosis Sanitarium .... ,423.18
Office expense Railroad Commissioners 1,183.89
State Law Library 2,746.46
Relief of T. R. Shaw 391.20
North Dakota Historical Society 8,273.86
Maintenance, Sub-Experiment Stations, Dickin-
    son, Langdon and Williston 12,333.16
Reimbursing Professor Ladd 2,171.23
St. Louis Exposition deficit 155.26
Contingency fund, Governor 405.65
Flags public buildings 159.74
Transportation patients Hospital Insane 23,528.55
Transportation convicts State Penitentiary....... 9,812.45
Transportation convicts Reform School 2,198.54
Expense Board of Management, State Normal
    Schools 819.24
Expense Board of Management, Mayville Normal
    School 862.32
Expense Board of Management, Valley City Nor-
    mal School 619.35
Per diem and expense Trustees:
    State University 1,462.00
    Agricultural College 3,094.70
    Industrial School 435.40
    Scientific School 791.95
    School of Forestry 561.20
    School for Deaf and Dumb 899.30
    State Penitentiary 2,872.50
    Reform School 2,289.38
    Hospital for Insane 885.55
    Institution for Feeble Minded 991.10
    Blind Asylum 668.90
    Soldiers' Home 436.20
Expense Supreme Court 2,605.50
Pure Paint law litigation 1,981.95
Fort Abercrombie State Park 214.25
Salary Conductor Teachers' Institutes 4,280.00
Board of Veterinary Medical Examiners 294.05
Live Stock Association 811.00
Relief of F. M. Baker 450.00
Maintenance and Building Fund, Public Health
    Laboratory, University 10,000.00
Building Fund, Hospital for Insane 102,242.49
Game and Fish Board of Control 20,561.03
Indemnity destruction glandered horses 81,687.33
State Library Commission 12,376.77
Live Stock Sanitary Board 22,739.32

Building Fund, Blind Asylum	28,042.50
Maintenance and Building Fund, Reform School	17,080.85
Maintenance and Building Fund, State Penitentiary	186,991.90
Fees, selecting U. and S. lands	147.90
Expense, selection indemnity lands	13.50
Expense, appraisement and sale U. and S. lands	11,542.89
Fire loss, State University	55.00
Refund elevator licenses	80.00
Salary teachers unorganized counties	80.51
White Stone Hills Battlefield .Commission	4,494.87
Armories for National Guard	20,170.00
State Poultry Association	600.00
Building fund, Agricultural College	116,488.92
Maintenance Edgeley Experimental Station	12,772.80
Building Fund, State University	109,085.79
Building Fund, Scientific School	58,693.74
Maintenance Fund, Scientific School	2,163.67
Expense Board U. and S. Lands	86,415.71
Advertising and expense, leasing U. and S. lands	2,681.63
North Dakota Aid Firemen's Association	8,000.00
Geological Survey:	
Agricultural College	1,000.00
State University	2,000.00
Maintenance and Building Fund, Industrial School	84,202.69
Military Fund, Industrial School	87.52
Lecturers, teachers' institutes	1,829.76
Jurisdiction over unorganized counties	8,375.10
State dipping tanks	87.50
Expense, farmers' institutes	20,787.40
Mileage and per diem, members Live Stock Sanitary Board	747.55
Langdon Experimental Station	10,000.00
Public Service Inquiry Commission	6.20
Traveling expense, Railroad Commissioners.....	1,385.85
Expense, Dairy Commisisoner	8,102.75
Traveling expense, State Oil Inspector	989.93
Expense, State Militia	48,497.94
Rock Island Military Reservation	1,420.38
Building Fund, School for Deaf	25,400.00
Building Fund, Mayville Normal School........	65,719.74
Maintenance and Building Fund, Valley City Normal School	89,127.03
Maintenance, Institution for Feeble Minded.....	94,449.89
Building Fund, School of Forestry	16,510.15
Personal expense, Railroad Commissioners......	1,499.97
Maintenance, Hospital for Insane	240,203.88

Total amount expended .... $ 2,543,374.71

CASH BALANCES.

	July 1, 1904	July 1, 1906	July 1, 1908	July 1, 1910
General fund	$ 239,769.42	$ 204,457.48	$ 262,907.89	$ 413,254.14
Asylum bond sinking fund	4,578.81	180.33	394.64	500.89
Bond trust fund	30,188.05	10,428.22	37,599.23	25,934.21
Fines, penalties and forfeitures	1,266.42	2,634.01	1,777.39	4,220.82
Half bounty fund	14,434.54	8,538.98	15,828.67	45,422.43
Coal test fund	18.86	1,408.78		
Oil inspection fund			49,454.24	38,872.48
Hotel inspection fund			289.83	309.21
Suspense cent			584.00	
State bond sinking fund	37,319.69	22,205.67	32,477.11	83,073.89
Disapproved land de, McLean unty		12,186.00		
Improvement und, Rock Island encampment grounds	89.95			
Armory fund, N. D. N. G.			2,000.00	
Twine and cordage plant—				
Operating	276.68	28,371.37	135.04	78,524.66
Construction	164.91	164.91	164.91	164.91
Sinking			27,647.53	25,180.34
Inst and income fund, common schools	34,968.57	82,357.82	30,161.10	101,183.87
Permanent fund, common schools	153,651.57	486,700.22	278,766.24	584,318.87
North Dakota Historical Society				177.00
Sinking fund—				
State University		9,407.00		
Agricultural College		9,407.40		
al School		4,083.32		
Reform School		3,762.96		
Soldiers' Hme		3,022.20		
ONE MILL TAX (EDUCATIONAL)				
State University	1,836.24	1,551.00	847.66	1,244.45
al College	918.11	775.48	510.33	750.46
Normal School, Valley City	551.01	465.28	380.36	560.20
Normal School, ale	551.01	564.28	330.93	486.92
School for Deaf and Dumb	596.70	504.11	48.70	231.33
School of Forestry			51.83	75.93
Industrial School	10,826.38	20,549.78	73.02	256.46
Academy of Science			9887	146.55

PERMANENT FUND

Institution				
State University	245.27	31,330.23	3,774.63	13,957.77
School of Mines	1,137.90	12,209.31	2,527.69	8,305.98
Agricultural College	96.37	70,491.13	21,646.01	22,213.49
Normal School, Valley City	1,334.05	11,703.48	1,767.98	28,259.20
Normal School, Mayville	1,673.53	10,669.30	5,165.35	13,815.07
School for Deaf and Dumb	2,330.71	14,927.78	2,481.77	10,793.17
Blind Asylum	346.59	7,636.68	3,640.04	11,404.31
School of Science	1,660.99	14,927.25	2,296.16	19,726.66
Industrial School	245.57	13,795.09	328.13	16,102.40
Reform School	643.60	16,145.91	6,225.74	9,418.69
Hospital for Insane	496.84	7,110.55	261.39	6,954.01
Soldiers' Home	1,458.19	14,113.87	804.42	4,878.35
Capitol Building	136.77	49,937.90	70,251.04	115,302.13
Power plant and trolley line	72.55			
Construction north wing	70,525.91			

INTEREST AND INCOME FUND

Institution				
State University	9,494.20	6,808.76	8,390.27	8,137.28
School of Mines	1,813.86	1,877.04	3,083.33	4,676.13
Agricultural College	7,412.44	12,535.30	13,585.16	32,957.26
Normal School, Valley City	7,254.28	3,789.53	3,646.83	4,945.70
Normal School, Mayville	2,514.67	2,124.74	2,331.51	2,853.89
School for Deaf and Dumb	2,135.31	2,703.99	4,946.00	3,411.13
Blind Asylum	9,076.74	12,094.93	2,406.47	3,572.49
School of Science	5,602.61	17,136.31	8,589.69	4,056.96
Industrial School	8,473.09	8,587.47	6,255.19	4,158.88
Reform School	3,156.51	9,523.04	14,946.10	21,917.27
Hospital for Insane	3,362.19	7,590.18	10,984.75	27,488.66
Soldiers' Home	12,051.64	2,609.94	2,426.70	4,231.65
Capitol Building	6,569.74	28,882.98	46,823.91	93,858.46
Total	$ 743,602.29	$ 1,305,190.29	$ 991,530.74	$ 1,902,296.51
Less overdraft	136.77		135.04	
Total cash balance	$ 743,465.52	$ 1,305,190.29	$ 991,395.70	$ 1,902,296.51

TAXES COLLECTED FROM COUNTIES.

July 1, 1908, to July 1, 1910.

Counties	General Fund	Asylum Bond Sinking Fund	Bond Interest Fund	Wolf Bounty Fund	One Mill Tax—Educational 1907	One Mill Tax—Educational 1906	State Bond Sinking Fund	Total
Adams	$ 11,915.94	$	$ 306.77	$ 628.03	$ 3,136.49		$ 316.43	$ 16,303.66
Barnes	71,239.58	$ 3.44	1,783.35	3,746.93	18,694.72	$ 39.17	1,876.31	97,373.50
Benson	44,613.36		1,079.06	2,347.86	11,622.34	115.31	1,175.05	60,952.98
Billings	27,056.51		687.21	1,417.97	6,308.30	14.88	710.60	36,195.47
Bottineau	63,145.24	.77	1,529.97	3,322.61	16,575.97	40.22	1,658.70	86,273.48
Bowman	11,811.39		302.46	615.61	3,108.23		310.80	16,148.49
Burleigh	42,699.68		1,084.72	2,247.64	11,077.24	163.70	1,118.01	58,381.99
Cass	149,673.29	17.50	3,824.29	7,860.83	39,043.03	237.04	3,938.66	204,594.64
Cavalier	53,479.99		1,236.06	2,814.75	13,964.72	109.18	1,399.70	73,004.40
Dickey	41,353.53	3.17	1,039.00	2,175.84	10,855.00	24.63	1,091.13	56,542.30
Dunn	11,552.85		283.95	607.91	3,040.13		303.88	15,788.72
Eddy	18,534.13		440.24	975.53	4,859.49	15.13	475.29	25,299.81
Emmons	26,174.99	.17	669.92	1,377.57	6,882.43	4.75	688.76	35,798.59
Foster	24,554.00		577.26	1,281.13	6,206.30	28.95	643.60	33,291.24
Grand Forks	99,961.03	12.37	2,504.28	5,248.65	26,116.56	117.43	2,623.83	136,584.15
Griggs	33,680.53	.04	820.64	1,772.58	8,837.53	24.62	885.00	46,020.94
Hettinger	12,845.96		307.87	676.12	3,380.48	19.26	338.07	17,548.50
Kidder	20,327.64	.71	511.89	1,068.68	5,325.32	65.85	526.17	27,779.67
La Moure	43,044.59	9.94	1,115.82	2,249.61	11,168.03	20.38	1,126.11	58,779.95
Logan	17,891.53	3.20	459.00	940.66	4,677.02		471.09	24,462.88
McHenry	54,032.94	.01	1,292.44	2,833.15	14,215.24	3.45	1,422.28	73,809.51
McIntosh	23,397.94		594.06	1,231.47	6,152.99	4.31	615.43	81,996.20
McKenzie	12,550.81	1.78	371.50	660.61	2,872.81	430.04	287.36	17,174.91
McLean	43,871.26	6.24	1,083.54	2,306.57	11,447.42	96.32	1,110.06	59,921.41
Mercer	11,112.07		276.33	584.58	2,797.82	126.30	199.86	15,096.96
Morton	54,824.49	9.59	1,389.48	2,878.34	14,152.47	246.43	1,451.37	74,952.17
Mountrail	10,538.62		277.19	554.60	2,772.48	.86	277.25	14,421.06
Nelson	38,364.87	.17	925.67	2,019.06	10,054.95	41.02	1,007.46	52,413.20

Oliver	7,859.02	....	191.78	413.64	2,060.33	7.77	206.08	10,788.62
Pembina	48,063.71	3.78	1,171.03	2,527.77	12,585.09	52.96	1,265.99	65,670.33
Pierce	29,641.25	....	709.28	1,559.96	7,778.48	21.06	779.11	40,489.14
Ramsey	50,827.01	....	1,242.49	2,675.11	13,204.78	171.04	1,324.44	69,444.87
Ransom	32,910.21	1.38	817.71	1,730.82	8,624.51	25.97	865.08	44,975.68
Richland	81,887.38	3.17	2,046.93	4,305.19	21,439.88	81.65	2,157.77	111,921.97
Rolette	27,870.54	8.89	688.36	1,460.58	7,182.41	119.42	734.13	38,064.33
Sargent	33,839.81	....	834.71	1,782.07	8,832.31	33.15	901.41	46,273.46
Sheridan	10,764.28	....	286.41	566.34	2,828.61	6.27	282.98	14,734.89
Stark	30,901.18	2.86	791.95	1,625.51	8,095.18	37.55	812.64	42,266.87
Stark (unorg.)	24.00	....	....	1.26	6.32	....	.64	32.22
Steele	32,087.63	.31	788.41	1,687.76	8,420.17	17.55	842.85	43,844.68
Stutsman	4,524.28	....	1,806.28	3,922.32	19,544.03	66.57	1,963.38	101,826.86
Towner	40,498.67	....	956.13	2,131.57	10,604.94	52.87	1,064.15	55,308.33
Traill	50,981.05	.10	1,279.87	2,683.22	13,408.36	6.87	1,341.36	69,700.83
Walsh	66,891.67	3.16	1,634.98	3,518.96	17,552.71	40.48	1,760.84	91,402.80
Ward	135,546.48	3.00	3,217.93	7,131.82	35,598.82	82.48	3,570.52	185,151.05
Wells	43,697.76	4.61	1,089.25	2,298.91	11,455.07	41.44	1,149.58	59,686.62
Williams	46,327.05	5.39	1,159.98	2,431.17	11,993.54	173.18	1,217.28	63,207.59
Total	$1,919,382.74	$105.75	$ 47,437.45	$100,908.93	$500,601.05	$ 3,027.51	$ 50,288.49	$ 2,621,651.92

FUNDS COLLECTED FROM COUNTIES

From July 1, 1908, July 1, 1910

| Counties | PERMANENT FUNDS OF THE STATE INSTITUTIONS | | | | | | |
| | State University | School of Mines | Agricultural College | Normal Schools | | School for Deaf | Hospital for Insane |
				Mayville	Valley City		
Adams			$ 720.00				
Barnes							
Benson	864.00		2,016.00	$ 93.00	$ 155.00	$ 897.92	$ 80.42
Billings							
Bottineau							
Bowman							
Burleigh							
Cass	11,051.07	12,302.85	16,706.43	7,446.76	12,144.58	7,475.79	6,243.81
Cavalier							
Dickey							
Dunn							
Eddy	4,328.00	432.00	2,427.21	753.00	1,255.00	2,011.44	773.60
Emmons	539.88	2,052.94	6,388.78	3,434.11	5,723.54	848.00	
Foster							
Grand Forks	120.00	120.00	1,016.00	300.43	500.71	480.00	320.00
Griggs							
Hettinger							
Kidder							
LaMoure	4.06						
Logan							
McHenry			1,088.00	1,020.00	1,700.00	2,280.00	900.00
McIntosh							
McKenzie							
McLean							
Mercer							
Morton							
Mountrail							

Nelson	2,618.73	1,240.06	2,851.16	526.31	877.18	1,039.14	480.00
Oliver							
Pembina							
Pierce							
Ramsey	7,129.45	2,584.00	9,914.52	1,199.36	1,998.95	1,245.59	1,564.93
Ransom							
Richland	1,344.00	1,685.42	53.10	156.96	261.60	1,172.00	
Rolette	2,895.16	1,845.72	8,539.80	620.76	1,034.63	1,724.10	188.80
Sargent		96.00	424.00			88.85	
Sheridan							
Stark							
Steele			384.00				
Stutsman	2,047.58	2,389.90	2,266.64	597.00	995.00	1,591.68	904.00
Towner	20,044.11	5,885.58	35,475.69	5,569.28	9,282.13	5,161.99	2,600.86
Traill			8,438.71	1,778.13	2,963.56	1,90.00	
/Wsh	3,689.36	832.00					
Ward							
Wells	6,950.15	3,002.58	7,874.90	1,929.94	3,216.58	1,135.62	224.00
Williams							
Total	$68,080.55	$33,869.05	$106,584.94	$25,425.04	$42,108.46	$29,112.12	$ 14,280.42

FUNDS COLLECTED FROM COUNTIES

From July 1, 1908, to July 1, 1909

PERMANENT FUNDS OF THE STATE INSTITUTIONS

Counties	Soldiers' Home	Blind Asylum	Industrial School	Scientific School	Capitol Building	Normal School	Total
Adams	400.00	.....	144.00	$.....	261.98	144.00	1,669.98
Bes	384.80	360.00	620.96	912.00	2,464.00	80.50	8,928.60
Benson							
Billings							
Bottineau							
Bowman							
Burleigh							
Cass	10,032.32	9,739.91	7,283.58	12,307.90	7,459.03	990.22	129,484.25
Cavalier							
Dickey							
Dunn							
Eddy	676.00	1,301.24	432.00	1,228.63	2,188.14	864.00	8,670.26
Emmons							
Foster	3,919.98	478.82	1,636.57	1,559.90	2,837.81	1,747.30	35,667.63
Grand Forks							
Griggs	160.00	657.00	2,277.04	289.00	340.00	544.00	6,804.78
Hettinger							320.00
Kidder							
LaMoure							4.06
Logan							
McHenry	2,888.41	.....	1,056.00	1,042.00		2,274.00	14,248.41
McIntosh							
McKenzie							
McLean							
Mercer							
Morton							
Mountrail							

Nelson	995.76	240.00	929.64	1,288.00	2,772.30	1,005.30	16,863.58
Oliver							
Pembina							
Pierce							
Ramsey	2,096.00	768.00	976.00	824.00	4,606.91	2,444.00	37,441.71
Ransom		80.00	256.00				336.00
Richland	384.00	440.00	800.00	1,056.00	1,405.42	504.00	8,662.50
Rolette	1,209.14	1,375.61	768.00	1,570.80	1,472.00	1,196.97	24,396.49
Sargent			l0.00				768.85
Sheridan							
Stark							
Steele							384.00
Stutsman	2,079.34	1,104.00	938.00	672.00	2,911.25	9000	19,416.39
Towner	6,468.35	3,973.33	10,095.19	6,968.55	82300	5,972.86	125,721.92
Traill							
Walsh	773.65	160.00	1,762.00	1,508.00	2,674.25	18032	27,620.98
Ward							
Wells	864.84		1,920.00	3,528.21	2,400.00	3,754.14	36,800.96
Williams							
Tbal	$33,332.59	$20,677.91	$32,055.58	$34,754.99	$42,107.09	$31,822.61	$514,211.35

FUNDS [DISTRIBUTED] [FROM] COUNTIES

From July 1, [19]08, to July 1, 1910

INTEREST AND INCOME FUNDS OF THE STATE INSTITUTIONS

Counties	State University	School of Mines	Agricultural College	Blind Asylum	Normal Schools — Mayville	Normal Schools — Valley City	School for Deaf
Adams	$ 35.00	$ 20.00	$ 25.00	$ 25.00	$ 8.83	$ 14.67	$ 13.25
Barnes	77.60	......	275.56	140.20	18.75	31.25	2.50
Benson	3,658.19	976.81	3,689.94	800.72	1,057.93	1,763.19	1,155.75
Billings				10.00			10.00
Bowman							
Burleigh	77.71	47.40	26.00		49.24	82.05	
Cass			19.25				
Cavalier	12,160.14	7,352.47	15,667.74	8,142.68	6,560.57	10,934.22	8,108.03
Dickey					2.10	3.50	
Dunn							
Eddy	1,924.78	285.04	1,421.96	559.49	445.25	742.06	841.02
Emmons	41.05	31.00	59.40	38.25	9.56	15.94	45.60
Foster	2,208.47	892.65	2,493.89	405.69	1,201.64	2,002.73	802.39
Grand Forks	579.92	22.40	420.35		93.91	118.00	311.52
Griggs	[1]36	29.76	348.62	177.94	141.07	233.82	174.04
Hettinger	58.08	71.21	160.20	76.76	26.81	44.69	75.00
Kidder							
LaMoure	1,549.22	1,188.42	2,142.29	1,088.99	419.24	698.71	884.81
Logan		46.00	96.00	8.00	24.00	40.00	32.00
McHenry	94.00	108.00	752.05	292.32	459.71	766.18	1,038.68
McIntosh	49.25	32.00	31.00	27.50	22.80	37.95	48.25
McKenzie							
McLean	429.65	27.50	343.32	160.00	74.68	124.48	45.50
Mercer			40.00	5.00	18.76	31.24	10.00
Morton	28.00	58.50	54.00	18.00	21.75	36.25	42.75
Mountrail							

County							
Nelson	2,644.10	985.50	4,124.51	636.93	787.52	1,312.50	1,481.13
Oler							
Pembina	9.60	10.00	7.50	1,173.88	2.64	1.86	
Pierce	4,105.01	1,090.01	5,931.22		1,075.81	1,792.99	1,416.59
Ramsey	14,732.35	5,062.74	21,696.13	2,872.98	3,785.89	6,309.85	3,296.48
Ransom		24.00		51.89	18.72	31.23	
Rlnd	464.06	276.26	171.79	236.72	45.08	75.13	403.36
Rolette	1,493.95	1,094.40	4,618.13	678.49	433.81	723.05	1,049.15
Sargent		53.34	217.94		6.07	10.13	45.66
Sheridan	236.65	76.88	414.32	29.75	72.95	121.58	50.85
Stark		10.00					
Steele	119.32	604.7	261.63	1,103.86	519.66	866.07	740.73
Stutsman	1,490.42	6,698.68	1,656.12	3,294.45	4,698.29	7,715.79	6,073.98
Trer	16,726.88		32,544.18				
Traill							
Walsh	3,927.73	1,332.32	5,722.34	58.60	1,881.57	3,135.92	1,042.68
Ward							
Valls	4,267.84	2,201.87	5,652.36	281.30	1,244.30	2,073.90	1,561.51
Williams							
Total	$73,379.33	$31,187.63	$111,084.74	$22,395.49	$25,282.91	$41,898.43	$30,803.21

FUNDS COLLECTED FROM COUNTIES

From July 1, 1908, to July 1, 1910

Counties	INTEREST AND INCOME FUNDS OF THE STATE INSTITUTIONS						Total
	Hospital for Insane	Soldiers' Home	Industrial School	Scientific School	Capitol Building	Reform School	
Adams	$ 13.25	$ 25.00	$ 25.00	$ 25.00	$ 20.00	$ 200	$ 270.00
Barnes		175.43	124.76	18.50	187.96	92.96	1,145.47
Benson	228.48	1,508.34	2,593.17	1,652.59	2,671.24	1,165.07	22,921.42
Billings			10.00	10.00	66.50		106.50
Bottineau							
Bowman							
Burleigh			5.00		115.20	158.93	561.53
Cass							19.25
Cavalier	4,318.82	7,113.11	8,990.57	8,783.64	12,344.01	6,772.80	1 1198.80
Dickey			15.00				20.60
Dunn							
Eddy	353.10	210.62	256.03	462.53	850.89	315.26	8,668.03
Emmons		70.00		12.80	54.00	21.00	501.60
Foster	708.48	1,286.38	983.81	725.64	2,187.47	1,551.35	17,450.69
Grand Forks	126.72		134.40	115.20	201.60	105.60	2,229.62
Griggs		146.24	640.14	111.45	94.32	380.31	2,685.07
Hettinger	229.60	81.30	98.82	89.33	253.00	75.00	1,339.80
Kidder							
LaMoure	489.60	1,616.39	930.64	1,075.30	2,686.77	1,097.44	15,867.82
Logan	16.00	8.00	29.00	28.00	109.00	16.00	452.00
McHenry	416.41	1,565.47	640.61	424.20	1,013.96	876.46	8,448.05
McIntosh		39.50	39.25	25.00	16.25		368.75
McKenzie							
McLean	30.00	91.00	118.00	93.75	196.00	49.50	18138
Mercer	7.50		15.00	5.00	358.00	10.00	500.50
Morton	39.25	65.75	28.00	44.00	37.50	53.25	527.00
Mountrail					28.75		2875

County							
Nelson	678.35	941.33	1,031.47	948.72	2,002.25	1,139.10	18,713.41
Oliver	2.50	2.50	1.25	5.00	11.25	19.40	76.00
Pembina	953.31	2,396.42	1,180.50	1,862.82	2,770.87	2,546.15	28,295.58
Pierce	2,967.32	-5,090.19	3,328.02	4,133.08	9,188.89	5,322.35	87,776.27
Ramsey		24.00	131.14	405.61	477.12	446.28	256.98
Ransom		98.46	207.20	989.30	1,581.89	914.62	3,346.69
Richland	39.62	719.01	392.86	30.20	350.00	30.00	14,775.45
Rolette	86.79		89.24	47.90	153.00	38.90	482.58
Sargent		50.00	35.00		120.66	10.00	1,532.28
Sheridan	17.50					227.64	173.00
Stark							729.25
Steele		970.20	1,107.76	1,022.52	1,541.33	447.98	12,980.67
Stutsman	407.85	5,558.64	8,209.21	7,219.65	11,645.06	5,699.70	117,893.72
Towner	1,809.21						
Traill							
Walsh	125.60	609.10	946.44	927.80	2,556.54	848.33	23,114.97
Ward					23.75		23.75
Wells	434.93	1,091.25	1,932.34	2,227.86	3,094.84	2,195.43	28,259.73
Williams							
Total	$14,500.19	$31,553.63	$34,269.63	$33,472.09	$58,993.62	$32,663.06	$541,424.96

FUNDS COLLECTED FROM COUNTIES

From July 1, 1908, to July 1, 1910

Counties	Interest and Income—Common		Schools	Permanent School Funds (Sales)	Fines, Penalties, and Forfeitures	Total
	Leasing	Interest on Sales	Hay Permits			
Adams	$ 3,402.60	$ 2,146.37		$	$ 337.89	$ 5,886.86
Barnes	3,003.80	64,902.12	$ 115.00	107,118.33	1,460.15	176,599.40
Benson	1,601.90	33,827.74	180.75	18,615.10	160.70	54,386.19
Billings	7,069.00	694.31		1,920.00	976.62	10,659.93
Bottineau	845.00	94,584.03	132.25	142,587.70	2,865.65	241,014.63
Bowman	2,990.00	4,067.76		4.00		7,061.76
Burleigh	4,233.80	10,462.47	220.00		2,095.75	17,012.02
Cass	16,103.17	30,287.03		53,096.24	4,376.15	103,862.59
Cavalier	1,141.45	75,178.70	219.50	85,346.33	160.75	162,046.73
Dickey	4,228.20	26,043.35			100.00	30,371.55
Dunn	4,231.00		56.00		102.00	4,333.00
Eddy	1,889.47	14,544.09	200.00	39,315.55	185.00	55,990.11
Emmons	6,138.85		209.00		1,899.44	8,238.29
Foster	1,832.05	30,142.26	223.00	32,533.83	182.42	64,913.56
Grand Forks	1,883.73	69,033.93		29,402.97		100,320.63
Griggs	2,065.75	19,727.08	35.00	45,845.99	500.00	68,173.82
Hettinger	3,257.00	4,687.09		7,322.00	10.00	15,276.09
Kidder	3,301.80		100.00		60.00	3,461.80
LaMoure	1,592.00	52,719.41	141.00	640.00	308.55	55,400.96
Logan	2,452.10	3,234.80	106.00			5,792.90
McHenry	4,085.10	49,127.33	110.00	71,153.60		124,176.03
McIntosh	3,060.00		117.00		120.00	3,297.00
McKenzie	3,370.20	834.03			307.05	4,511.28
McLean	7,505.40	5,073.37	310.00		1,430.94	14,319.71
Mercer	2,790.00	53.90	10.00			2,853.90
Morton	9,130.05	4,576.00			1,540.25	15,246.30
Mountrail	2,113.65				995.00	3,108.65
Nelson	509.00	33,250.26	25.00	49,799.62	136.60	83,730.48

Oliver	1,811.00				55.00	1,866.00
Pembina	421.60	23,649.32		22,739.81	309.90	47,120.63
Pierce	2,839.50	22,535.49	47.50		146.00	25,568.49
Ramsey	924.50	54,911.24	116.25	32,957.92	1,151.80	90,061.71
Ransom	875.00	38,226.32	45.00	83,034.45	393.00	122,573.37
Richland	2,620.51	48,453.96	5.00	65,232.52	150.70	116,462.69
Rolette	899.95	22,827.95	129.50	43,787.13	28.25	67,672.78
Sargent	1,796.30	42,518.97	5.00	75,879.45	594.50	120,794.22
Sheridan	3,401.75	999.78			648.75	5,050.28
Stark	3,318.34				319.80	3,638.14
Steele	5,408.10	30,854.26	30.00	81,080.28	326.35	117,698.99
Stutsman	3,203.67	51,010.77	304.00	65,901.20	501.60	120,921.24
Towner	1,316.60	43,364.19	226.25	46,126.23	424.85	91,458.12
Traill	2,970.59	20,133.82		24,908.34	67.15	48,079.90
Walsh	777.85	36,988.74	167.00	49,275.05	838.30	88,046.94
Ward	8,558.95	84,119.48		229,016.08	3,164.07	324,858.58
Wells	1,819.25	43,003.57	408.50	64,033.74	1,191.00	110,456.06
Williams	6,894.24				1,445.05	8,339.29
Total	$155,683.77	$1,192,805.29	$ 3,784.50	$1,588,583.06	$ 32,156.98	$ 2,973,013.60

FOLLOWING IS GIVEN A COMPARISON STATEMENT SHOWING
COLLECTIONS.

RECEIVED FROM	PERIOD		
	July 1, 1904 to July 1, 1906	July 1, 1906 to July 1, 1908	July 1, 1908 to July 1, 1910
Taxes	$1,208,221.32	$1,501,432.43	$1,919,282.74
Secretary of State, inc. tax	31,658.50	35,942.75	37,976.00
Secretary of State, fees....	19,834.75	26,973.06	28,686.75
Commissioner of Insurance	156,017.28	204,531.20	173,892.00
Clerk Supreme Court......	2,822.15	2,135.15	2,266.75
Comm'r Agricul. and Labor	3,186.00	2,089.25	1,786.00
Public Examiner	10,305.00	15,685.70	19,518.10
U. and S. lands, fees......	29,422.10	27,058.40	44,163.00
Interest on public funds....	41,139.01	70,670.90	82,481.67
Elevator licenses	7,154.00	23,855.00	21,752.00
Trolley fares	3,794.47	5,249.70	5,342.00

ONE MILL TAX.

PAYMENTS MADE TO	PERIOD	
	July 1, 1906 to July 1, 1908	July 1, 1908 to July 1. 1910
Academy of Science	$ 6,772.22	$ 19,976.36
Agricultural College	79,348.29	100,475.44
Industrial School	11,851.35	34,958.63
Normal School, Mayville	49,301.98	65,279.32
Normal School, Valley City	52,688.12	75,267.53
State University	146,845.39	165,992.25
School for Deaf and Dumb	39,724.96	30,350.42
School of Forestry	30,642.71	10,077.19

INTEREST AND INCOME.

PAYMENTS MADE TO	PERIOD	
	July 1, 1906 to July 1, 1908	July 1, 1908 to July 1910
Academy of Science	$32,980.59	$ 44,456.23
Agricultural College	90,431.56	109,034.05
Blind Asylum	37,148.53	25,355.72
Capitol building	30,518.51	12,126.17
Hospital for Insane	8,390.00	8.43
Industrial School	29,034.12	41,534.57
Normal School, Mayville	18,321.34	28,787.42
Normal School, Valley City	31,359.93	47,316.30
Reform School	22,338.10	30,004.30
School for Deaf and Dumb	21,676.46	37,080.26
Soldiers' Home	28,087.88	35,134.76
State University	62,801.96	85,546.37

TAX COLLECTIONS TO THE CREDIT OF THE GENERAL FUND.

1903	$ 502,372.54
1904	534,219.34
1905	618,555.62
1906	645,667.25
1907—Taxes, $723,340.81; miscellaneous, $396,279.32...	1,119,620.13
1908—Taxes, $770,508.25; miscellaneous, $238,804.71...	1,009,312.96
1909—Taxes, $883,921.98; miscellaneous, $401,909.62...	1,285,831.60

STATE TUITION FUND.

July 1, 1904, to July 1, 1906.

Apportionment Quarter Ending	Number of Children Enumerated	Interest and Income—Common Schools		Fines, Penalties and Forfeitures		Total Amount Apportioned	Rate Total Per Capita
		Amount Apportioned	Rate Per Capita	Amount Apportioned	Rate Per Capita		
8- 1-1904	118,812	$ 52,277.28	$ 0.44	$ 1,188.12	$ 0.01	$ 53,465.40	$ 0.45
9-12-1904	100	44.00	0.44	1.00	0.01	45.00	0.45
2- 1-1905	120,268	108,241.20	0.90	1,202.68	0.01	09,443.88	0.91
4-30-1905	120,268	173,191.68	1.44	2,405.44	0.02	175,597.12	1.46
8- 1-1905	126,326	58,109.96	0.46	3,789.78	0.03	61,899.74	0.49
11- 1-1905	126,439	60,690.72	0.48	2,538.78	0.02	63,219.50	0.50
1-31-1906	126,487	06,249.08	0.84	2,529.74	0.02	108,778.82	0.86
4-30-1906	126,487	23,881.99	1.77	5,059.48	0.04	228,941.47	1.81
	865,187	$ 782,685.91		$ 18,705.02		$ 801,390.93	

July 1, 1906, to July 1, 1908.

Apportionment Quarter Ending	Number of Children Enumerated	Interest and Income—Common Schools		Fines, Penalties and Forfeitures		Total Amount Apportioned	Rate Total Per Capita
		Amount Apportioned	Rate Per Capita	Amount Apportioned	Rate Per Capita		
8- 1-1906	80,461	$ 20,691.50	$ 1.50	$ 3,218.44	$ 0.04	$ 123,909.94	$ 1.54
11- 1-1906	80,500	29,785.00	0.37	4,830.00	0.06	34,615.00	0.43
2- 1-1907	80,519	72,467.10	0.90	1,610.38	0.02	74,077.48	0.92
5- 1-1907	80,874	84,086.24	3.76	2,426.22	0.03	306,512.46	3.79
8- 1-1907	132,979	73,88.45	0.55	5,309.16	0.04	78,547.61	0.59
*8- 1-1907				10.00	0.04	10.00	
11- 1-1907	133,166	19,974.90	0.15	2,663.32	0.02	22,638.22	0.17
1-31-1908	133,835	64,240.80	0.48	2,676.70	0.02	66,917.50	0.50
4-31-1908	134,300	33,209.00	2.63	4,029.00	0.03	357,38.00	2.66
	856,634	$1,037,692.99		$ 26,773.22		$1,064,466.21	

July 1, 1908, to July 1, 1910.

Date		$	%	$	%	$	%
7-11-1908	20	130.60	6.53	3.00	0.15	133.60	6.58
7-31-1908	143,089	94,438.74	0.66	2,861.78	0.02	97,300.52	0.68
**8-31-1908	58	38.28	0.66	1.16	0.02	39.44	0.68
10-31-1908	143,227	22,916.32	0.16	1,432.27	0.01	24,348.59	0.17
1-31-1909	143,472	101,865.12	0.71	2,869.44	0.02	104,734.56	0.73
5- 1-1909	143,578	182,344.06	1.27	4,307.34	0.03	186,651.40	1.30
7-31-1909	148,683	383,602.14	2.58	2,973.66	0.02	386,575.80	2.60
11- 1-1909	148,717	90,717.37	0.61	4,461.51	0.03	95,178.88	0.64
2- 1-1910	148,717	102,614.73	0.69	2,974.34	0.02	105,589.07	0.71
5- 1-1910	148,758	602,469.90	4.05	7,437.90	0.05	609,907.80	4.10
	1,168,319	$1,581,137.26		$ 29,322.40		$1,610,459.66	

* Account error.   ** Special.

1897.

Real estate ....,...............	$	62,816.904
Personal property		20,920.559
Railroad		7,985,527
Telephone		
Telegraph		
Express		
Street Railway		

Total assessed valuation all property 1897 .. $ 91,722,990

THE LEVY 1897.

General fund	3.8 mills
Wolf bounty	.1 mills
Bond. interest	.5 mills
Total levy 1897	4.4 mills

1898.

Real estate	$	65,458,290
Personal property		22,929,831
Railroad		12,869,355
Telephone		
Telegraph ...., ..:...............		
Express		
Street Railway		

Total assessed valuation all property 1898 .. $ 101,257,476

THE LEVY 1898.

General fund	3.8 mills
Wolf bounty	.1 mills
Bond interest	.5 mills
Total levy 1898	4.4 mills

1899.

Real estate	$	72,110,059
Personal property		25,209,411
Railroad		17,014,958
Telephone .....,:..........		
Telegraph ....:.............		
Express		
Street Railway ·...........·.........................		

Total assessed valuation all property 1899 .. $ 114,334,428

THE LEVY 1899.

General fund	3.8 mills
Wolf bounty	.2 mills
Bond interest	.5 mills
Total levy 1899 ....:...	4.5 mills

1900.

Real estate .... $ 73,574,494
Personal property 26,262,466
Railroad 17,367,525
Telephone ....
Telegraph ....
Express ....
Street Railway ....

    Total assessed valuation all property 1900 .. $ 117,204,485

THE LEVY 1900.

General fund ....:..... .... 3.8 mills
Wolf bounty .... .2 mills
Bond interest .... .5 mills

    Total levy 1900 .... 4.5 mills

ASSESSED VALUATION, STATE OF NORTH DAKOTA, 1901.

Real estate .... $ 77,996,178
Personal property 28,085,797
Railroad property 17,983,367
Express companies 139,220
Telephone lines 108,017
Telegraph companies 287,290

    Total assessed valuation of all property 1901 $ 124,599,869
    Total acreage assessed 1901 19,427,965

THE LEVY 1901.

General fund .... 4.0 mills
Bond interest .... .5 mills
Wolf bounty .... .2 mills
Asylum bond sinking fund .... 1.4 mills
Educational institution tax .... 1.0 mills

    Total levy .... 7. mills

1902.

Real estate .... $ 85,433,334
Personal property 27,962,089
Railroad property 19,985,989
Express companies 144,423
Telephone companies 135,115
Telegraph companies 219,426

    Total assessed valuation of all property 1902 $ 133,880,376
    Total acreage assessed 1903 21,116,859

THE LEVY 1902.

General fund .... 4. mills
Bond interest fund .... .3 mills
State bond sinking fund .... .2 mills
Educational institution fund .... 1. mills

    Total levy .... 5.5 mills

1903.

Real estate	$	91,616,090
Personal property		33,059,799
Railroad property		21,307,242
Express companies		145,591
Telephone companies		190,630
Telegraph companies		218,092

Total assessed valuation of all property 1903	$	146,537,444
Total acreage assessed 1903		21,403,435

THE LEVY 1903.

General fund	3.8 mills
Wolf bounty. fund	.2 Mills
Bond interest fund	.2 mills
State bond sinking fund	.3 mills
Educational institution tax	1. mills
Total levy	5.5 mills

1904.

Real estate	$	98,355,197
Personal property		34,314,634
Railroad property		21,160,304
Express companies		154,168
Telephone companies		296,402
Telegraph		224,564

Total assessed valuation of all property 1904	$	155,505,269

THE LEVY 1904.

General fund	3.6 mills
Wolf bounty fund	.2 mills
Bond interest fund	.1 mills
State bond sinking fund	.6 mills
Educational institution tax	1. mills
Total levy	5.5 mills

1905.

Real estate	$	113,127,196
Personal property		37,097,598
Railroad property		22,477,987
Telegraph property		207,917
Telephone property		466,650
Express property		156,154
Street railway property		17,575

Total assessed valuation of all property 1905	$	173,551,077
Total acreage assessed 1905		25,876,974

TAX LEVY 1905.

General fund	3.8 mills	$	659,494
Wolf bounty fund	.2 mills		34,710
Bond interest fund	.3 mills		52,065
Educational institution tax	1. mills		173,551
Total levy	5.3 mills	$	919,820

1906.

Real estate	$	125,323,154
Personal property		42,029,884
Railroad property		27,949,152
Telephone property		593,902
Express property		196,916
Street railway		25,195
Private car lines		89,100

Total assessed valuation of all property 1906	$	196,462,584
Total acreage assessed 1906		27,538,347

TAX LEVY 1906.

General fund	3.8 mills	$	746,557
Wolf bounty fund	.2 mills		39,292
Bond interest fund	.3 mills		58,938
Educational institution tax	1. mills		196,462
Total levy	5.3 mills		$1,041,251

1907.

Real estate	$	137,034,644
Personal		45,807,627
Railroad		29,213,973
Telegraph		273,130
Telephone		684,684
Street railway		29,070
Express		254,414

Total assessed valuation of all property 1907	$	213,297,542
Total acreage assessed 1907		27,844,159

THE LEVY 1907.

General fund	3.8 mills	$	810,531
Wolf bounty	.2 mills		42,659
Mill tax (educational)	1. mills		213,297
State bond sinking	.1 mills		21,330
Total levy	5.1 mills		$1,087,817.

1908.

Real estate	$	147,147,963
Personal		47,368,847
Railroads		33,068,881
Telephone		623,237
Express		273,788
Street railway		29,070
Telegraph		255,476

Total assessed valuation of all property 1908	$	228,767,262
Total acreage assessed 1908		30,955,531

THE LEVY 1908.

General fund	3.8 mills	$	869,315
Wolf bounty	.2 mils		45,753
Mill tax (educational)	1. mills		228,767
State bond sinking	.1 mills		22,876

Bond interest	.1 mills	22,876
Total levy	5.2 mills	$1,189,589

1909.

Real estate	$	184,124,702
Personal property		54,442,525
Railroads		40,255,261
Express companies		317,863
Telegraph companies		293,136
Street railways		39,134
Telephone companies		942,079
Total assessed valuation all property 1909..	$	278,414,200
Total acreage assessed 1909		33,017,438

THE LEVY 1909.

General fund	3.8 mills	$1,057,973
Wolf bounty fund	.2 mills	55,682
Mill tax (educational)	1. mills	278,414
State bond sinking	.1 mills	27,841
Bond interest	.1 mills	27,841
Total levy	5.2 mills	$1,447,751

1910.

Real estate	$	184,589,989
Personal property		51,909,379
Railroad property		40,276,266
Express companies		359,713
Telegraph companies		325,833
Street railways		58,980
Telephone companies		1,074,033
Total assessed valuation for all property 1910	$	278,594,193
Total acreage assessed 1910		34,394,240

THE LEVY 1910.

General fund	3. mills	$ 835,782
Wolf bounty	.2 mills	55,718
Mill tax (educational)	1. mills	278,594
State bond sinking	.1 mills	27,859
Bond interest	.1 mills	27,859
Total levy	4.4 mills	$1,225,812

INSURANCE CARRIED ON STATE INSTITUTIONS.

Agricultural college	$	629,750.00
Biological station		4,250.00
Blind Asylum		45,000.00
Capitol building		242,000.00
Executive mansion		7,400.00
Fish hatchery		5,000.00
Hospital for Insane		410,000.00
Industrial school		70,200.00
Institution for Feeble Minded		69,800.00
Mayville Normal School		145,500.00
Mining Experiment Station		4,000.00

```
Penitentiary ...............................        153,000.00
Reform School .............................         31,500.00
School for Deaf and Dumb ...................        76,550.00
School of Forestry .........................        27,000.00
Soldiers' Home .............................        26,700.00 .
State University ...........................       407,633.00
Valley City Normal School ..................       176,000.00
```

Total .... $ 2,531,283.00

TWO PER CENT INSURANCE TAX PAID TO FIRE DEPARTMENTS

Year	Towns	Amount
1901	42	$ 6,894.27
1902	48	7,136.97
1903	58	9,057.81
1904	63	9,912.25
1905	63	9,816.75
1906	71	11,100.90
1907	74	14,181.56
1908	75	15,134.76
1909	93	17,094.22
1910	105	19,743.66

Insurance on Public Buildings, July 1, 1908 to July 1, 1910,
cost .... $ 36,423.11
Amount of insurance carried on State Institutions $2,531,283.00

INDEX.

Lightning Source UK Ltd.
Milton Keynes UK
UKHW032254141118
332327UK00005B/177/P